English History Trivia

Unlock the Pivotal Moments and Intriguing Characters of English History with 500 Interactive Questions and Answers

Welcome Aboard, Check Out This Limited-Time Free Bonus!

Ahoy, reader! Welcome to the Ahoy Publications family, and thanks for snagging a copy of this book! Since you've chosen to join us on this journey, we'd like to offer you something special.

Check out the link below for a FREE e-book filled with delightful facts about American History.

But that's not all - you'll also have access to our exclusive email list with even more free e-books and insider knowledge. Well, what are ye waiting for? Click the link below to join and set sail toward exciting adventures in American History.

Access your bonus here

https://ahoypublications.com/

Or, Scan the QR code!

Table of Contents

Introduction

Throughout the centuries, England has been at the forefront of major historical events that have shaped not only its own destiny but also that of the entire world. From royal scandals and political upheavals to scientific breakthroughs and cultural revolutions, there is no shortage of captivating tales from this small yet mighty country. In this introduction, we invite you to join us on a journey through time as we unlock some of the most pivotal moments and characters in English history. But unlike your typical history lesson, we will be exploring these stories in a fun and interactive way—through trivia questions!

Our collection includes 500 thought-provoking questions that cover various periods in English history. These questions are designed for kids but can be enjoyed by all ages. They are perfect for family game nights or educational activities in schools.

So why should you care about English history? Well, for one thing, it is full of enough drama and intrigue to rival any Hollywood blockbuster. From bloody battles between kings to secret affairs between queens, the stories of English history are filled with scandal and excitement. But beyond the entertaining aspects, studying history allows us to learn from past mistakes and understand how they have shaped our present.

Our trivia questions cover a wide range of topics, including monarchs, famous battles, important inventions and discoveries, cultural movements, and more. By answering these questions, you will not only expand your knowledge of English history but also gain insights into its impact on the world we live in today. But this is not just about testing your historical knowledge—it's about discovering lesser-known facts that may surprise even the most avid history buff. Did you know that Queen Victoria was an excellent pianist? Or that King Henry VIII had six wives? Through our trivia questions, you will discover fascinating details about influential figures such as William the Conqueror and Margaret Thatcher, while learning about events like the Miners' Strike or The Blitz.

So, whether you are a history enthusiast or just looking for some fun facts to impress your friends, our English history trivia book has something for everyone. We hope that this journey through time will not only pique your interest in English history but also inspire you to delve deeper into its rich and complex past. So, grab a pen and paper, gather your family or friends, and let's dive into the world of English history trivia!

Prehistoric England

This chapter will explore the fascinating history of prehistoric England. Discover how people lived during this period with limited resources and developed complex trade networks between themselves and neighboring nations! Gain insight into the lives of our prehistoric ancestors and find out what life was like before written records were kept in Britain.

1. What type of animal is commonly associated with prehistoric England?

    A. Woolly mammoth

    B. Saber-toothed tiger

    C. Wooly rhinoceros

    D. Giant sloth

2. What became the primary source of food for Britain during the Late Neolithic period?

    A. Hunting and gathering

    B. Farming and herding livestock

    C. Trading for food supplies

    D. Fishing in the ocean

3. Why was Stonehenge built during the prehistoric period?

    A. To create a sacred space for religious rituals

    B. For burials or memorials

    C. As defensive structures against invading armies

    D. To mark important astronomical events

4. What type of material were prehistoric tools made from?

   A. Iron

   B. Bronze

   C. Stone

   D. None of the above

5. What was the name of the land bridge that joined Britain to Europe ca. 14,000 years ago?

   A. Britannia

   B. Doggerland

   C. Pangea

   D. None of the above

6. Which of these statements is true about prehistoric Britain?

   A. A land bridge never existed between Britain and Ireland

   B. Britain was colonized by immigrants from southern Italy

   C. We know who built Stonehenge

   D. All of the above

7. When did the construction of Stonehenge begin according to archeologists?

   A. Fifth century BCE

   B. Late fourth millennium BCE

   C. 6000 BCE

   D. None of the above

8. What type of animal was domesticated in prehistoric England?

   A. Wolves

   B. Cats

   C. Sheep

   D. Elephants

9. Stonehenge is considered which of these?

   A. Monolith

   B. Cist

   C. Dolmen

   D. Megalith

10. What type of people are believed to have built Stonehenge?

    A. The Celts

    B. The Saxons

    C. The Druids

    D. We don't know

11. How did early farmers in Britain improve their agricultural techniques during the Neolithic period?

    A. By developing irrigation systems

    B. By advancing their tools

    C. By introducing new crops from other regions

    D. By using fertilizers to increase crop yields

12. What were the members of the ancient priestly class in Britain called?

    A. Druids

    B. Magi

    C. Rabbi

    D. Brahmins

13. Around when did Britain become part of the Atlantic trade system?

    A. 2000 BCE

    B. 1700 BCE

    C. 1300 BCE

    D. 600 BCE

14. What did early farmers in Britain use to plow their fields?

    A. Horses

    B. Donkeys

    C. Oxen

    D. Sheep

15. Which culture rose to prominence in Western Europe during the Late Bronze Age?

    A. Frankish

    B. Roman

    C. Celtic

    D. British

16. With which other region was Britain most culturally alike in the first millennium BCE?

A. Greece

B. France

C. Italy

D. Scythia

17. Western European societies during the Late Bronze Age are placed under which predominant archeological culture?

A. Hallstatt culture

B. Funnelbeaker culture

C. Clovis culture

D. None of the above

18. When did Iron Age begin in Britain?

A. 1000 BCE

B. 800 BCE

C. 500 BCE

D. 300 BCE

19. Which of these is considered one of the main archeological pieces of ancient Celtic art found in Britain?

A. Rosetta Stone

B. Battersea Shield

C. Sutton Hoo Helmet

D. None of the above

20. What event is typically considered the end of the British Iron Age?

A. Anglo-Saxon migration

B. Roman invasion

C. Late Iron Age collapse

D. British Civil War

21. Which of the following Iron Age buildings are found in large numbers in Britain?

A. Hillforts

B. Mastabas

C. Pyramids

D. Starforts

22. Which of these ancient historians first mentions Britain in his writings?

    A. Pytheas of Massalia

    B. Thucydides

    C. Diodorus Siculus

    D. Livy

23. Which of these tribes is thought to have invaded Britain ca. 300 BCE?

    A. The Boii

    B. The Galatians

    C. The Parisii

    D. The Danes

24. What is the oppidum?

    A. An early English legal code

    B. A large, fortified Iron Age settlement

    C. A type of temple found in Scotland

    D. None of the above

25. What year is the Snettisham Hoard dated to?

    A. 150 BCE

    B. 100 BCE

    C. 70 BCE

    D. 30 BCE

Answers

1. A. Woolly mammoth
2. B. Farming and herding livestock
3. D. To mark important astronomical events
4. C. Stone
5. B. Doggerland
6. A. A land bridge never existed between Britain and Ireland
7. B. Late fourth millennium BCE
8. C. Sheep
9. D. Megalith
10. D. We don't know
11. B. By advancing their tools
12. A. Druids
13. C. 1300 BCE
14. C. Oxen
15. C. Celtic
16. B. France
17. A. Hallstatt culture
18. B. 800 BCE
19. B. Battersea Shield
20. B. Roman invasion
21. A. Hillforts
22. A. Pytheas of Massalia
23. C. The Parisii
24. B. A large, fortified Iron Age settlement
25. C. 70 BCE

The Romans in England
(55 BCE–410 BCE)

This chapter will explore the history of the Romans in England. We will discover how they brought significant economic, political, and social change to the region during their occupation, which lasted for almost five centuries. We'll explore how their presence influenced all aspects of life in England and look at some of the most important figures from this period.

26. What was the Roman province of Britain called?

 A. Britannia

 B. Romania

 C. Provincia Romana

 D. Britannicus

27. What did the Romans call the native Britons?

 A. Saxons

 B. Kalends

 C. Celts

 D. Picts

28. What is the name of the bridge originally built by the Romans across the River Thames?

 A. Boudicca Bridge

 B. Hadrian's Bridge

 C. Tower Bridge

 D. London Bridge

29. How many times did Julius Caesar invade Britain?

    A. Once

    B. Twice

    C. Three times

    D. Four times

30. When was the first Roman invasion of Britain organized?

    A. 63 CE

    B. 59 BCE

    C. 55 BCE

    D. 49 BCE

31. When was the conquest of Britain concluded?

    A. 43 CE

    B. 31 BCE

    C. 65 CE

    D. None of the above

32. Why is the *Commentarii de Bello Gallico* significant in regard to British and English history?

    A. It is considered the earliest written document about British history

    B. It was written by an unknown early British king

    C. It contains the earliest mention of Britain in a foreign source

    D. None of the above

33. Who is the author of the *Commentarii de Bello Gallico*?

    A. Bede

    B. Livy

    C. Thucydides

    D. Julius Caesar

34. What was the outcome of the Boudican uprising?

    A. Total Roman defeat

    B. Roman retreat from Britain

    C. A failed attempt at liberating Britain from Roman rule

    D. None of the above

35. When did the Boudican revolt take place?

    A. 26-27 CE

    B. 60-61 CE

    C. 75-76 CE

    D. 103-104 CE

36. Who was Boudica?

    A. The claimant to the British throne

    B. The legendary ancestor of King Arthur

    C. The warrior-queen of the Britons

    D. The Roman general who joined the Britons

37. Which of these Roman emperors constructed a defensive fortification in northern Britain to mark the extent of Roman rule?

    A. Claudius

    B. Nero

    C. Theodosius

    D. Hadrian

38. Who fought against the Romans during their conquest of Britain?

    A. The Picts

    B. The Celts

    C. The Belgae

    D. All of the above

39. What was the main export of early Roman Britain?

    A. Agricultural products

    B. Metals

    C. Pottery

    D. None of the above

40. Which of these was the earliest capital of Roman Britain?

    A. York

    B. Colchester

    C. Caernarvon

    D. London

41. What became Britain's biggest port when the Romans were there?

    A. Dover

    B. London

    C. Bristol

    D. Colchester

42. What were the civitas?

    A. Administrative divisions of Roman Britain

    B. The court system of Roman Britain

    C. Governor's personal bodyguards in Roman Britain

    D. Both a and b

43. What caused the end of Roman rule in Britain?

    A. Invasions of the Angles and Saxons

    B. Worsening relations with Rome

    C. Internal revolt

    D. All of the above

44. Approximately how many people lived in Roman Britain by the late third century, during the peak of Roman rule?

    A. one million

    B. two million

    C. three million

    D. five million

45. Who is considered the first British Christian martyr?

    A. St. Nicholas

    B. St. Alban

    C. St. George

    D. None of the above

46. What language did most of the British population speak on an everyday basis during Roman rule in Britain?

    A. Latin

    B. Angle

    C. Brittonic

    D. Celtic

47. Which Roman general expanded Roman rule in Britain as far north as Caledonia?

    A. Tacitus

    B. Agricola

    C. Gnaeus

    D. Gracchus

48. Which of these emperors reformed the administrative structure of Britain during their reign in 197 CE?

    A. Claudius

    B. Marcus Aurelius

    C. Trajan

    D. Septimius Severus

49. Which emperor introduced the office of the *vicarius* to Britain with his administrative reforms?

    A. Justinian

    B. Diocletian

    C. Antoninus Pius

    D. Caracalla

50. What was the responsibility of a *vicarius*?

    A. He was the supreme justice of the province

    B. He was the most important official in the province

    C. He was the deputy military chief of the province

    D. None of the above

51. What did **Emperor** Antoninus Pius do to try to keep the Picts out of Roman Britain?

    A. Built a wall

    B. Offered a trade deal

    C. Established centers of exchange on the border

    D. None of the above

52. **When** did Rome withdraw from Britain?

    A. 400 CE

    B. 405 CE

    C. 407 CE

    D. 410 CE

53. What was the main problem Rome experienced in Britain during the fourth and early fifth centuries?

    A. A series of rebellions

    B. The migration of northern tribes into the south

    C. A ten-year plague

    D. None of the above

54. Where was most of the Roman influence concentrated in Britain?

    A. West

    B. Southwest

    C. Center and east

    D. North

55. Which Roman emperor may have declined to send assistance to Britain in the early fifth century?

    A. Honorius

    B. Arcadius

    C. Theodosius

    D. Constantius

Answers

26. A. Britannia
27. C. Celts
28. D. London Bridge
29. B. Twice
30. C. 55 BCE
31. A. 43 CE
32. A. It is considered the earliest written document about British history
33. D. Julius Caesar
34. C. A failed attempt at liberating Britain from Roman rule
35. B. 60-61 CE
36. C. The warrior-queen of the Britons
37. D. Hadrian
38. D. All of the above
39. B. Metals
40. B. Colchester
41. B. London
42. A. Administrative divisions in Roman Britain
43. D. All of the above
44. C. three million
45. B. St. Albam
46. C. Brittonic
47. B. Agricola
48. D. Septimius Severus
49. B. Diocletian
50. B. He was the most important official in the province
51. A. Built a wall
52. D. 410 CE
53. A. A series of rebellions
54. C. Center and east
55. A. Honorius

Early Medieval England (410 BCE–1066 CE)

In the early medieval period of 410 BCE-1066 CE, England experienced many changes. People left their small villages for new towns or cities and built castles to protect them. Kings became powerful rulers, and Christianity started to spread. Peasants tilled the soil, farmers kept their herds, and merchants and traders traveled far and wide. It was a fascinating time full of new experiences and discoveries!

56. What type of government existed in early medieval England?

   A. Monarchy

   B. Communism

   C. Democracy

   D. Autocracy

57. In what year did William the Conqueror become the ruler of England?

   A. 1040 CE

   B. 1100 CE

   C. 1066 CE

   D. 1085 CE

58. How many battles were fought by Alfred the Great during his campaign in 871?

A. 5

B. 7

C. 3

D. 9

59. From where did the Anglo-Saxons primarily migrate to England?

A. Western France

B. Northern Germany and the Low Countries

C. Northern Iberia

D. Western Scandinavia

60. What language did the population of England start to speak after the Anglo-Saxon migration?

A. Old English

B. Late Brittonic

C. Latin

D. Middle English

61. Who began to increasingly invade England from the late eighth century?

A. The Franks

B. The Vikings

C. The Irish

D. The Spanish

62. Which famous English king issued The Great Charter, or Magna Carta, in 1215 CE?

A. Alfred the Great

B. William I

C. Henry II

D. John

63. Who was the first Anglo-Saxon king to convert to Christianity according to the *Ecclesiastical History of the English People*?

A. Alfred the Great

B. Æthelbert of Kent

C. Edward the Confessor

D. Henry I

64. How many kingdoms did the Anglo-Saxon migrants eventually establish in England?

A. 3

B. 4

C. 6

D. 7

65. How are the Anglo-Saxon kingdoms of early Middle Ages England commonly referred to?

A. Heptarchy

B. Pentarchy

C. Triarchy

D. None of the above

66. Which of these was an Anglo-Saxon kingdom?

A. Wessex

B. Kent

C. East Anglia

D. All of the above

67. In what year did the Battle of Hastings take place?

A. 1041 CE

B. 1066 CE

C. 1086 CE

D. 1100 CE

68. King Penda was a prominent ruler of which of these Anglo-Saxon kingdoms?

A. Northumbria

B. Wessex

C. Mercia

D. Kent

69. When year did the "Great Heathen Army" invade England?

    A. 865 CE

    B. 870 CE

    C. 878 CE

    D. 881 CE

70. Who led the English against the Vikings at the Battle of Edington?

    A. Alfred the Great

    B. William the Conqueror

    C. Edward the Confessor

    D. Æthelbert

71. Which monastery did the Vikings attack in 793?

    A. Kent

    B. Lindisfarne

    C. York

    D. Lincoln

72. Until when did Alfred the Great rule England?

    A. 865 CE

    B. 886 CE

    C. 889 CE

    D. 899 CE

73. What was the name of the tribute paid to the Vikings by the Englishmen?

    A. Burh

    B. Scandpenny

    C. Danegeld

    D. None of the above

74. What was the name of the king who ruler Denmark, Norway, and England until his death in 1035?

    A. Æthelbert of Kent

    B. Cnut the Great

    C. Harald Hardrada

    D. William the Conqueror

75. Which English city became the center of the Danish presence in England in 867?

A. Kent

B. York

C. Lincoln

D. Stratfordshire

76. Which Viking managed to conquer and become the king of England for five weeks in 1013?

A. Cnut the Great

B. Thorkell

C. Sweyn Forkbeard

D. Gurthu

77. Who was the author of the famous work *Ecclesiastical History of the English People*?

A. Alfred the Great

B. Monke Nene

C. The Venerable Bede

D. None of the above

78. Which of the Anglo-Saxon kingdoms managed to unite England in 927?

A. Northumbria

B. East Anglia

C. Mercia

D. Wessex

79. Who became the first ing of the English in 927?

A. Edward the Confessor

B. Alfred the Great

C. Æthelstan

D. Offa

80. Who emerged victorious from the Battle of Stamford Bridge in 1066?

A. Harald Hardrada

B. Harold Godwinson

C. Neither side

D. None of the above

81. Where was William I crowned the king of England?

A. Westminster Abbey

B. The Tower of London

C. Buckingham Palace

D. St. Paul's Cathedral

82. What was the name of the manuscript produced by William the Conqueror after the survey of the English population in the late eleventh century?

A. The Norman Cofex

B. The Great Charter

C. The Domesday Book

D. None of the above

83. Under which of these kings did the Kingdom of Mercia reach the height of its power?

A. Offa

B. Ceolred

C. Peada

D. Eowa

84. Who was the last crowned king of England before the invasion of William the Conqueror?

A. Edward the Confessor

B. Harold Godwinson

C. Harald Hardrada

D. Ecbert

85. Who succeeded Alfred the Great on the throne of England after his death?

    A. Æthelstan

    B. Edward the Elder

    C. Edgar

    D. Eadred

Answers

56. A. Monarchy
57. C. 1066 CE
58. D. 9
59. B. Northern Germany and the Low Countries
60. A. Old English
61. B. The Vikings
62. D. John
63. B. Æthelbert of Kent
64. D. 7
65. A. Heptarchy
66. D. All of the above
67. B. 1066 CE
68. C. Mercia
69. A. 865 CE
70. A. Alfred the Great
71. B. Lindisfarne
72. D. 899 CE
73. C. Danegeld
74. B. Cnut the Great
75. B. York
76. C. Sweyn Forkbeard
77. C. The Venerable Bede
78. D. Wessex
79. C. Æthelstan
80. B. Harold Godwinson
81. A. Westminster Abbey
82. C. The Domesday Book
83. A. Offa
84. B. Harold Godwinson
85. B. Edward the Elder

Medieval England and the Norman Conquest (1066–1485)

In 1066, England began a period known as the Middle Ages, which lasted more than 400 years. Medieval England was a time of castles, knights, and grand feasts. Kings and queens reigned, and battles were fought on the plains and in the cities. Lords and ladies gathered in the court to discuss important matters. People lived in small towns and villages and traveled on dirt roads. Join us as we uncover the secrets of medieval England—a fascinating time when history was made.

86. Who fought in the Battle of Hastings?

    A. The English and the French

    B. The Danes and the Swedes

    C. The Normans and the Saxons

    D. The Scots and the Irish

87. How was the English social system organized during the Middle Ages?

    A. It was a theocracy

    B. It was a merchant oligarchy

    C. It was a feudal monarchy

    D. It was a republic

88. What religion did most people in medieval England practice?

   A. Judaism

   B. Christianity

   C. Islam

   D. Pagan

89. Who was king of England from 1066-1087?

   A. Henry I

   B. William the Conqueror

   C. John I

   D. Richard I

90. On what day was William the Conqueror crowned as king?

   A. May 14

   B. October 13

   C. December 25

   D. January 1

91. What is the name of a series of campaigns waged by the Normans after the conquest in northern England to deal with local rebellions?

   A. Harrying of the North

   B. Massacre of Northumbria

   C. The Northern Crusade

   D. None of the above

92. What was the Magna Carta?

   A. A charter of trade rules

   B. A document setting out the rights and privileges of the church

   C. A treaty between the pope and the kings of England

   D. An agreement between the king and the barons of England, setting out basic rights

93. What formal title did William hold before conquering England?

   A. Count

   B. Duke

   C. King

   D. Lord

94. Who inherited the kingdom after the death of William the Conqueror?

    A. William II

    B. Robert

    C. James I

    D. John I

  95. In medieval England, how was someone declared an outlaw?

    A. By sentence of an ecclesiastical court

    B. By fleeing the kingdom

    C. By declaring bankruptcy

    D. By sentence of a feudal court

96. What is the period of English history between 1138 and 1153 also known as?

    A. The Time of Troubles

    B. The Anarchy

    C. The First Civil War

    D. The Crisis

97. Who was the first of the Angevin rulers of England?

    A. Robert

    B. Stephen de Blois

    C. Henry I

    D. Henry II

98. Which of these kings inherited the French provinces of Anjou and Normandy and later acquired Aquitaine through marriage?

    A. Henry II

    B. Richard I

    C. Henry III

    D. George I

99. Which house formed the short-lived Angevin Empire, which included territories of England and France in the twelfth and the thirteenth centuries?

A. Westminster

B. Normans

C. Plantagenets

D. Stuarts

100. Which English king participated in the Third Crusade?

A. John I

B. Henry II

C. Richard I

D. Richard II

101. Which of these English kings managed to lose many of the French possessions?

A. Eleanor of Aquitaine

B. John I

C. Richard I

D. Richard III

102. Which of these English kings was captured by Simon de Montfort during the Second Barons' War in 1264?

A. Richard II

B. Edward I

C. Henry III

D. Henry IV

103. What did guilds mainly do in the Middle Ages?

A. Contributed funds to the church

B. Set labor standards and wages

C. Lend money to the royal family

D. None of the above

104. Who defeated Simon de Montfort at the Battle of Evesham?

A. Edward I

B. Henry III

C. Roger Mortimer

D. Edward II

105. What year is considered the beginning of the Hundred Years' War between England and France?

A. 1330

B. 1337

C. 1339

D. 1341

106. Why did the Hundred Years' War break out?

A. Edward III was assassinated by the French

B. French nobles wanted to undermine the English monarchy

C. Edward III claimed the French throne

D. All of the above

107. Who did Edward the Black Prince capture in 1356, after the Battle of Poitiers?

A. His father, Edward III

B. King John II of France

C. Chateau Josselin

D. None of the above

108. At which battle did the English decisively defeat the French in 1415?

A. Calais

B. Orleans

C. Agincourt

D. Rouen

109. What was the main strength of the English army during the medieval period?

A. Heavy cavalry

B. Innovative artillery

C. Pikemen

D. Longbowmen

110. Who emerged victorious from the Hundred Years' War?

A. England

B. France

C. Neither side

D. We don't know

111. Which English king was deposed in 1399?

    A. Richard II

    B. Richard III

    C. Henry IV

    D. Henry V

112. How are the series of civil wars in England that began in 1455 referred to?

    A. The Game of Thrones

    B. The Wars of the Claimants

    C. The Wars of the Roses

    D. The Struggles of the Yorks

113. Who was the king when the civil war began?

    A. Henry IV

    B. Henry V

    C. Henry VI

    D. Henry VII

114. What was one of the main reasons for England's instability in the mid-fifteenth century?

    A. A new plague

    B. Economic problems caused by the Hundred Years' War

    C. Unstable line of succession in the House of Plantagenet

    D. Riots in London and York

115. Which two cadet houses of the House of Plantagenet vied for power at the beginning of the civil war?

    A. Tudor and Hannover

    B. York and Hannover

    C. Westminster and Tudor

    D. York and Lancaster

Answers

86. C. The Normans and the Saxons
87. C. It was a feudal monarchy
88. B. Christianity
89. B. William the Conqueror
90. C. December 25
91. A. Harrying of the North
92. D. An agreement between the king and the barons of England, setting out basic rights
93. B. Duke
94. A. William II
95. D. By sentence of a feudal court
96. B. The Anarchy
97. D. Henry II
98. A. Henry II
99. C. Plantagenets
100. C. Richard I
101. B. John I
102. C. Henry III
103. B. Set labor standards and wages
104. A. Edward I
105. B. 1337
106. C. Edward III claimed the French throne
107. B. King John II of France
108. C. Agincourt
109. D. Longbowmen
110. B. France
111. A. Richard II
112. C. The Wars of the Roses
113. C. Henry VI
114. B. Economic problems caused by the Hundred Years' War
115. D. York and Lancaster

The Tudors (1485–1603)

Four hundred years ago was a time of revolution in England. This period is known as the Tudor period. It began with the coronation of King Henry VII in 1485 and continued until Queen Elizabeth I's death in 1603. During this time, the Tudors changed England forever, creating a powerful and unified nation. Grand palaces were built, explorers discovered new lands, and books were printed for the first time. It was a time of adventure and intrigue filled with examples of bravery, ambition, power, and love. In this chapter, dive into the era of the Tudors and discover England's way of life during this period.

116. Which English king had six wives?

    A. Henry VIII

    B. Edward VII

    C. George III

    D. Charles I

117. The Tudors were descendants of a noble family from which kingdom?

    A. England

    B. Ireland

    C. Spain

    D. Wales

118. Who was the founder of the Tudor dynasty?

   A. Edward VI

   B. Henry VII

   C. Charles I

   D. George III

119. Which English king signed the Treaty of Troyes—an agreement during the Hundred Years' War that would have made him inherit the throne of France?

   A. Henry V

   B. Edward VI

   C. Henry VI

   D. John II

120. When did the War of the Roses end?

   A. 1479

   B. 1480

   C. 1485

   D. 1487

121. Who took the throne after Elizabeth I, ending the Tudor dynasty?

   A. James I

   B. Edward VI

   C. Charles I

   D. Henry VII

122. Who managed to briefly seize power in England before being defeated by Henry VII?

   A. Henry VI

   B. Richard III

   C. Charles I

   D. Oliver Cromwell

123. What was the last significant battle of the War of the Roses?

   A. Agincourt

   B. Deorham

   C. Brunanburh

   D. Bosworth Field

124. With which European kingdom did England forge an alliance in the fourteenth century that lasted for hundreds of years and is still ongoing?

A. Spain

B. Portugal

C. Poland

D. Italy

125. Who were the parents of Elizabeth I?

A. Henry VIII and Anne Boleyn

B. Edward VI and Jane Seymour

C. Henry VII and Catherine Parr

D. Charles I and Anne Boleyn

126. How did Elizabeth I earn the nickname "The Virgin Queen"?

A. By refusing to marry

B. By staying in her castle

C. By joining a convent

D. By wearing white dresses

127. When did Henry VII die?

A. 1505

B. 1507

C. 1509

D. 1511

128. The Act of Supremacy declared the English sovereign to be the supreme head of what?

A. The Church of England

B. The Catholic Church

C. The British Empire

D. The British Parliament

129. The Church of England was created by which English king?

A. Henry VIII

B. Henry IX

C. Charles I

D. Charles II

130. Over what Christian doctrine did the English Reformation initially break with Catholicism?

A. Prohibition of adultery

B. Prohibition of divorce

C. Prohibition of alcohol

D. Prohibition of priestly marriage

131. Who was executed for treason in 1536?

A. Mary Queen of Scots

B. Lady Jane Grey

C. Elizabeth I

D. Anne Boleyn

132. Which monarch reversed many of the Protestant policies of their predecessors after rising to the throne of England in 1553?

A. Elizabeth I

B. Mary I

C. Edward VI

D. Charles I

133. Who succeeded the throne of England in 1547 after the death of Henry VIII?

A. Edward V

B. Henry IX

C. Edward VI

D. Elizabeth I

134. Which kingdom's king did Mary marry in 1556?

A. Portugal

B. Spain

C. France

D. Denmark

135. Who came to the throne after the death of Mary I?

A. Elizabeth I

B. Charles I

C. John II

D. Edward VII

136. How were Elizabeth I and Mary, Queen of Scots, related?

A. They were sisters

B. They were mother and daughter

C. They were cousins

D. They were not related

137. The Elizabethan period coincided with which major artistic movement?

A. Baroque

B. Classical

C. Gothic

D. Renaissance

138. What was one of the main achievements of Elizabeth I's reign?

A. Expansion into France

B. End of domestic religious conflicts

C. Development of trade with China

D. Reformation of the Parliament

139. With which nation did England go to war during the late 1580s?

A. Portugal

B. Spain

C. France

D. Denmark

140. When did the Spanish Armada attack England?

A. 1569

B. 1588

C. 1590

D. 1591

141. The defeat of the Spanish Armada resulted in what?

A. The English becoming independent

B. The recognition of England as a major European power

C. A rise in trade with other countries

D. Catherine of Aragon becoming queen of England

142. Who was the last Tudor monarch?

   A. Mary Tudor

   B. Edward VI

   C. Elizabeth I

   D. Henry VIII

143. Which admiral led the English forces in defeating the Spanish Armada?

   A. Ralph Dalaval

   B. John Paveley

   C. Francis Drake

   D. None of the above

144. When did Elizabeth I die?

   A. 1600

   B. 1602

   C. 1603

   D. 1605

145. What treaty ended the Anglo-Spanish War?

   A. The Peace of Tilsit

   B. The Treaty of London

   C. The Peace of Dover

   D. The Treaty of Madrid

Answers

116. A. Henry VIII
117. D. Wales
118. B. Henry VII
119. A. Henry V
120. C. 1485
121. A. James I
122. B. Richard III
123. D. Bosworth Field
124. B. Portugal
125. A. Henry VIII and Anne Boleyn
126. A. By refusing to marry
127. C. 1509
128. A. The Church of England
129. A. Henry VIII
130. B. Prohibition of divorce
131. D. Anne Boleyn
132. B. Mary I
133. C. Edward VI
134. B. Spain
135. A. Elizabeth I
136. C. They were cousins
137. D. Renaissance
138. B. End of domestic religious conflicts
139. B. Spain
140. B. 1588
141. B. The recognition of England as a major European power
142. C. Elizabeth I
143. C. Francis Drake
144. C. 1603
145. B. The Treaty of London

The Protestant Reformation in England (1517–1684)

The Protestant Reformation began in Germany in 1517 and quickly reached England. This movement had an enormous impact on politics, religion, and culture during this period. Protestants challenged traditional beliefs about God, faith, and worship, leading to changes in how people practiced their faith. The English monarchy also changed this era, with rulers like Henry VIII introducing new religious practices into the country. By 1684, the Protestant Reformation had ended, but it left behind a legacy still seen today!

146. What event marked the beginning of the Protestant Reformation?

    A. Martin Luther's 95 Theses

    B. King Henry VIII's divorce from Catherine of Aragon

    C. Queen Elizabeth I's ascension to the throne

    D. John Wycliffe's translation of the Bible into English

147. Who was considered the leader of the Protestant Reformation in England?

    A. Jan Hus

    B. Thomas Cranmer

    C. John Calvin

    D. King James I

148. Which king founded the Anglican Church?

A. Henry VII

B. Henry VIII

C. Edward VI

D. Elizabeth I

149. Which of these was part of the Act of Uniformity?

A. To provide equal rights to Catholics and Protestants

B. To create a single, unified church among Catholics and Protestants

C. To establish an English Bible in every parish

D. To require everyone to attend mass weekly

150. How did the Puritans view religious ceremonies?

A. They believed them to be necessary for salvation

B. They felt they should be done with as much pomp and ceremony as possible

C. They only approved of simple, meaningful rituals

D. They rejected all religious ceremonies

151. What were some long-term consequences of the Protestant Reformation in England?

A. Increased economic prosperity

B. Forced conversion to Catholicism

C. Burning of Bibles

D. Increased power for Roman Catholic priests

152. What was the purpose of William Laud's policies?

A. To restore divine order

B. To increase royal control over church matters

C. To reduce restrictions on nonbelievers

D. To promote toleration between Catholics and Protestants

153. Which organization was formed to move away from the Church of England?

A. The Congregationalists

B. The Quakers

C. The Anglicans

D. The Puritans

154. Who wrote *The Pilgrim's Progress,* one of the most influential works during the Protestant Reformation in England?

    A. Thomas More

    B. John Bunyan

    C. William Tyndale

    D. Martin Luther

155. How did Queen Elizabeth I respond to religious differences within her kingdom?

    A. She executed anyone who challenged her authority

    B. She allowed freedom of worship but imposed restrictions on any religion that threatened her rule

    C. She tried to mediate between the Church of England and Roman Catholics

    D. None of the above

156. What did the Test Act of 1673 require?

    A. That all citizens be tested for literacy

    B. That all citizens take a loyalty oath to the Church of England

    C. That all Roman Catholics pay an additional tax

    D. That only Anglicans could hold public office

157. What was the "High Church" during The Protestant Reformation in England?

    A. A church where services were held in Latin and conducted by priests wearing elaborate vestments

    B. A church that focused on treating Protestants like second-class citizens

    C. An emphasis on strict orthodoxy, religious ritualism, and episcopal government

    D. An effort to move away from hierarchical authority structures within the Church of England

158. Under which ruler was the prominence of Roman Catholicism briefly restored in England?

    A. Mary I

    B. Elizabeth I

    C. Edward VI

    D. Oliver Cromwell

159. What did the Toleration Act of 1689 allow for during the Protestant Reformation in England?

A. Non-Anglicans to hold public office

B. Conversion from Catholicism to Anglicanism

C. Religious freedom for all denominations except Catholics

D. Freedom of worship within certain limits

160. Under King James I, which Christian denomination did Scotland mostly adhere to?

A. Protestantism

B. Catholicism

C. Orthodoxy

D. Methodism

161. What was the significance of the Thirty-nine Articles?

A. To proclaim spiritual independence from Rome

B. To serve as a declaration of faith for Anglicans

C. To provide equal rights to Catholics and Protestants

D. To create a single, unified church

162. How did King Charles I respond to religious differences within his kingdom?

A. He tried to impose uniformity on all denominations

B. He allowed freedom of worship but imposed restrictions on any religion that threatened his rule

C. He abolished the Church of England

D. He promoted toleration for all religious denominations

163. Who wrote *The Book of Common Prayer* during the Protestant Reformation in England?

A. Thomas Cranmer

B. John Wycliffe

C. William Tyndale

D. Martin Luther

164. What did the Elizabethan Settlement accomplish during the Protestant Reformation in England?

    A. It required everyone to attend mass weekly

    B. It established an English Bible in every parish

    C. It created a single, unified church

    D. It established tolerance of different religious beliefs

165. What was the purpose of John Calvin's teachings during the Protestant Reformation in England?

    A. To promote a return to Catholic orthodoxy

    B. To increase royal control over Church matters

    C. To restore divine order

    D. To emphasize humans' responsibility for their own salvation

166. Who led one of the most influential movements toward reform within the Church of England and became archbishop of Canterbury in 1533?

    A. William Tyndale

    B. Martin Luther

    C. John Wycliffe

    D. Thomas Cranmer

167. What was the purpose of King James I's King James Bible during the Protestant Reformation in England?

    A. To promote tolerance between Catholics and Protestants

    B. To have a new version of the Bible in English

    C. To tax those who did not adhere to Protestantism

    D. None of the above

168. Who were the Recusants in England during the Reformation?

    A. Followers of Elizabeth

    B. An underground extreme Protestant group

    C. Roman Catholics who refused to attend mandatory services of the Anglican Church

    D. None of the above

169. How did most Catholic priests and bishops initially respond to Puritan efforts?

A. They supported them wholeheartedly

B. They tolerated their presence but disagreed with their views

C. They persecuted Puritan views

D. They tried to mediate between different denominations

170. Who wrote the *Institutes of The Christian Religion*?

A. William Tyndale

B. John Bunyan

C. Martin Luther

D. John Calvin

Answers

146. A. Martin Luther's 95 Theses

147. B. Thomas Cranmer

148. B. Henry VIII

149. C. To establish an English Bible in every parish

150. C. They only approved of simple, meaningful rituals

151. A. Increased economic prosperity

152. B. To increase royal control over church matters

153. D. The Puritans

154. B. John Bunyan

155. B. She allowed freedom of worship but imposed restrictions on any religion that threatened her rule

156. D. That only Anglicans could hold public office

157. C. An emphasis on strict orthodoxy, religious ritualism, and episcopal government

158. A. Mary I

159. D. Freedom of worship within certain limits

160. A. Protestantism

161. B. To serve as a declaration of faith for Anglicans

162. A. He tried to impose uniformity on all denominations

163. A. Thomas Cranmer

164. D. It established tolerance of different religious beliefs

165. D. To emphasize humans' responsibility for their own salvation

166. D. Thomas Cranmer

167. B. To have a new version of the Bible in English

168. C. Roman Catholics who refused to attend mandatory services of the Anglican Church

169. C. They persecuted Puritan views

170. D. John Calvin

The Stuart Dynasty (1603–1714)

The Stuart dynasty resided over an exciting period in British history. It came to power in England when King James VI of Scotland became King James I of England in 1603, uniting the two countries and creating what is now known as Great Britain. For the next 111 years, members of this powerful family ruled England, Scotland, and Ireland. They brought a wealth of knowledge from their Scottish homeland and used it to create new laws that favored all people regardless of class or background. This period also witnessed notable advances in science, literature, and art!

171. When was the Stuart dynasty founded?

    A. 1594

    B. 1603

    C. 1371

    D. 1714

172. What religion were most of the Stuarts?

    A. Protestant

    B. Catholic

    C. Christian

    D. Jewish

173. What happened to King Charles I during his reign as leader?

A. He abdicated

B. He was exiled

C. He was executed

D. He died in battle

174. When did Queen Anne become ruler of England, Scotland, and Ireland?

A. 1603

B. 1702

C. 1714

D. 1688

175. Who was the last monarch in the Stuart dynasty?

A. James II

B. Queen Anne

C. Charles I

D. Elizabeth I

176. What event caused King James II to be removed from power?

A. The Glorious Revolution

B. Gunpowder Plot

C. War of Spanish Succession

D. English Civil War

177. How many children did Mary, Queen of Scots, have?

A. 1

B. 2

C. 3

D. 4

178. Which religion was favored by King Charles I?

A. Protestantism

B. Catholicism

C. Baptism

D. Judaism

179. Where did Prince Charles Edward Stuart die?

A. London

B. Scotland

C. France

D. Italy

180. Which of these rulers ascended the throne in 1660?

A. James I

B. Charles II

C. Elizabeth I

D. Mary, Queen of Scots

181. What did King Charles I do to start a civil war?

A. He tried to diminish the role of the Parliament

B. He wanted to invade Spain

C. He raised taxes

D. He imposed religious reforms

182. When did The English Bill of Rights take place?

A. 1603

B. 1702

C. 1688/9

D. 1714

183. Who defeated James II at Battle of Boyne in Ireland?

A. William III

B. George III

C. Anne

D. James IV

184. Where did the Battle of Boyle take place?

A. Scotland

B. The Netherlands

C. England

D. Ireland

185. Why did the English nobility dislike James II?

    A. He had abolished the Parliament

    B. He had been a Catholic

    C. He had raised their taxes

    D. None of the above

186. Who was Mary, Queen of Scots' son?

    A. Charles I

    B. Charles II

    C. James VI and I

    D. Henry VIII

187. When did the English Civil War begin?

    A. 1633

    B. 1642

    C. 1649

    D. 1645

188. When did William and Mary take the throne?

    A. 1603

    B. 1702

    C. 1714

    D. 1688

189. Who was the last Catholic monarch of England?

    A. Charles II

    B. Charles I

    C. James VI and I

    D. Mary II

190. Who was the oldest son of James I and Anne of Denmark?

    A. George III

    B. William of Orange

    C. Henry Frederick

    D. Mary, Queen of Scots

Answers

171. C. 1371
172. B. Catholic
173. C. He was executed
174. B. 1702
175. B. Queen Anne
176. A. The Glorious Revolution
177. A. 1
178. B. Catholicism
179. D. Italy
180. B. Charles II
181. A. He tried to diminish the role of the Parliament
182. C. 1688/9
183. A. William III
184. D. Ireland
185. B. He had been a Catholic
186. C. James VI and I
187. B. 1642
188. D. 1688
189. C. James VI and I
190. C. Henry Frederick

English Civil War (1642–1651)

The English Civil War was a time of great unrest in England. Between 1642 and 1651, two groups fought against each other: the Royalists, who wanted to keep the king in power, and the Parliamentarians, who wanted more rights for ordinary people. Both sides used powerful weapons like cannons and muskets as they battled on land and at sea. In the end, the Parliamentarians won, but not without paying a heavy price—many lives were lost during this devastating war!

191. What caused the English Civil War?

    A. A disagreement between King Charles I and Parliament

    B. A battle fought between England and Scotland

    C. An argument among members of Parliament about religion

    D. None of the above

192. Which side was victorious in the English Civil War?

    A. The Royalists led by King Charles I

    B. The Roundheads led by Oliver Cromwell

    C. Neither—it ended in a draw

    D. The Scots under William Wallace

193. Who wrote "The Leveller Manifesto" during the English Civil War?

    A. Thomas Hobbes

    B. John Lilburne

    C. James Harrington

    D. William Penn

194. What years are referred to as the "Personal Rule" of Charles I?

    A. 1625-1628

    B. 1630-1648

    C. 1629-1640

    D. 1640-1648

195. Who was the father of Charles I?

    A. James VI and I

    B. James VII and II

    C. Henry VIII

    D. None of the above

196. Who was the leader of the Royalists during the English Civil War?

    A. Oliver Cromwell

    B. Charles I

    C. Henry VIII

    D. None of the above

197. What kind of government did Oliver Cromwell set up after winning the war?

    A. A constitutional monarchy

    B. An absolute monarchy

    C. A republic based on religious principles

    D. A protectorate with a range of executive powers

198. When did the Battle of Marston Moor take place?

    A. 1640

    B. 1641

    C. 1642

    D. 1644

199. Who emerged victorious from the Battle of Naseby?

    A. Charles I

    B. Cromwell

    C. Prince William

    D. Neither side

200. What was the name of the standing force established by the Parliamentarians during the First Civil War?

    A. Army for Freedom

    B. Liberty Corps

    C. New Model Army

    D. None of the above

201. When did the second stage of the English Civil War begin?

    A. 1650

    B. 1644

    C. 1648

    D. None of the above

202. What was the charge against Charles I that led to his execution?

    A. Mismanagement of royal treasury

    B. Treason

    C. Regicide

    D. Heresy

203. When did the Anglo-Scottish War begin?

    A. 1649

    B. 1650

    C. 1651

    D. 1652

204. When did the Parliamentarian army achieve victory over the Royalists at the battle of Preston?

    A. 1648

    B. 1642

    C. 1549

    D. 1776

205. What year did King Charles I surrender to Scottish forces and start negotiations for a peace treaty with the Roundheads?

    A. 1645

    B. 1647

    C. 1649

    D. None of these

Answers

191. A. A disagreement between King Charles I and Parliament
192. B. The Roundheads led by Oliver Cromwell
193. B. John Lilburne
194. C. 1629-1640
195. A. James VI and I
196. B. Charles I
197. D. A protectorate with a range of executive powers
198. D. 1644
199. B. Cromwell
200. C. New Model Army
201. C. 1648
202. B. Treason
203. B. 1650
204. A. 1648
205. B. 1647

The Commonwealth of England (1649–1660)

The Commonwealth of England was a period in British history from 1649 to 1660. It began when King Charles I was overthrown and the government changed to rule without a king or queen. During this era, England worked hard for peace and prosperity, laying foundations that still shape life today. People had new opportunities to express themselves through trade, religious freedom, literature, and art!

206. What was the Commonwealth of England?

    A. A constitutional monarchy

    B. A republic led by Oliver Cromwell

    C. An oligarchy

    D. All of the above

207. Why did the English government decide to create the Commonwealth of England?

    A. To restore the monarchy

    B. To stabilize after the civil war

    C. To increase trade

    D. To overthrow Parliament

208. What was abolished during the Commonwealth of England?

A. Monarchy

B. Religion

C. Slavery

D. All of the above

209. How did Oliver Cromwell's rule differ from that of previous rulers in England?

A. He increased taxes for all citizens

B. He implemented strict religious laws

C. He created more freedom and liberty than before

D. He brought temporary peace and unity among the people

210. What kind of structure did Oliver Cromwell's government most resemble during the Commonwealth?

A. Absolute monarchy

B. Constitutional monarchy

C. Parliamentary democracy

D. Military rule

211. What religion was favored in the Commonwealth?

A. Catholicism

B. Judaism

C. Protestantism

D. Islam

212. What was Oliver Cromwell's title during the Commonwealth?

A. Prime Minister

B. King

C. President

D. Lord Protector

213. Who succeeded Oliver Cromwell as leader of England following his death in 1658?

A. Richard Cromwell

B. James II

C. William III and Mary II

D. Elizabeth I

214. How were laws enforced by the government during the Commonwealth period?

A. With strict punishments

B. With negotiation and compromise

C. Through religious laws

D. With the help of local militias

215. What effect did the Commonwealth have on the economy of England?

A. It weakened it

B. It strengthened it

C. It had no impact

D. It caused inflation

216. How many lord protectors were there for the duration of the Commonwealth?

A. One

B. Two

C. Three

D. Four

217. Which of the following statements is true?

A. The Commonwealth diminished the authority of the king

B. The Commonwealth helped decrease taxes on the commoners

C. The Commonwealth managed to expand in England's colonies

D. The Commonwealth was ultimately a great success

218. What happened in 1660?

A. Oliver Cromwell died

B. The Commonwealth was attacked by France

C. Monarchy was restored

D. None of the above

219. Who was crowned king in Westminster Abbey in April 1661?

A. James VIII

B. Charles II

C. Richard Cromwell

D. William III

220. When was the Declaration of Breda issued?

A. April 1660

B. December 1660

C. May 1659

D. March 1658

Answers

206. B. A republic led by Oliver Cromwell
207. B. To stabilize after the civil war
208. A. Monarchy
209. D. He brought temporary peace and unity among the people
210. C. Parliamentary democracy
211. C. Protestantism
212. D. Lord Protector
213. A. Richard Cromwell
214. B. With negotiation and compromise
215. B. It strengthened it
216. D. Four
217. A. The Commonwealth diminished the authority of the king
218. C. Monarchy was restored
219. B. Charles II
220. A. April 1660

The Age of Enlightenment in England (1685–1815)

The Age of Enlightenment in England was a period from the late seventeenth to the mid-nineteenth century. It was when many people questioned traditional beliefs and began to think more critically about the world around them. During this era, famous philosophers such as John Locke, Isaac Newton, and David Hume helped bring revolutionary ideas to light that changed how we look at the world today!

221. Which major movement immediately preceded the Age of Enlightenment?

A. The Renaissance

B. The Scientific Revolution

C. The Industrial Revolution

D. The Age of Discovery

222. Which of these philosophers was influential during the Age of Enlightenment in England?

A. John Locke

B. Voltaire

C. Karl Marx

D. Thomas Hobbes

223. Why did some people refer to this period as "the Age of Reason"?

A. Because it was a time when science and logic were used to solve social problems

B. Because religious beliefs had been abolished

C. Because political systems had changed significantly

D. Because social conventions were relaxed

224. Who wrote the widely read book *An Essay Concerning Human Understanding*?

A. John Locke

B. Thomas Hobbes

C. Voltaire

D. Karl Marx

225. Which country is considered the birthplace of the Age of Enlightenment?

A. England

B. France

C. Germany

D. Italy

226. Which of these is a purpose of the scientific method greatly developed during the Enlightenment?

A. To disprove theories

B. To refute arguments

C. To create hypotheses

D. All of the above

227. Which of these philosophers are known as the "social contract" theorists?

A. Jean-Jacques Rousseau

B. John Locke

C. Thomas Hobbes

D. All of the above

228. Who is considered the "Father of Capitalism" and a leading Scottish scholar from the Enlightenment?

A. Thomas Hobbes

B. Adam Smith

C. Karl Marx

D. Jean-Jacques Rousseau

229. Who is the author of *Leviathan*?

A. Adam Smith

B. John Locke

C. Thomas Hobbes

D. Jean-Jacques Rousseau

230. What new ideas emerged during the Age of Enlightenment?

A. Capitalism

B. Socialism

C. Liberalism

D. All of the above

231. Which of these was not the main focus of early Enlightenment thinkers?

A. Social reform

B. Political change

C. Religious toleration

D. Emancipation of slaves

232. Which English thinker produced *The History of the Decline and Fall of the Roman Empire*?

A. Thomas Hobbes

B. John Locke

C. Edward Gibbon

D. Anthony Collins

233. Who wrote *On Liberty*?

A. John Stuart Mill

B. Adam Smith

C. Oliver Cromwell

D. Voltaire

234. What metaphorical significance does the Leviathan carry in *Leviathan*?

A. God

B. All-powerful ruler

C. Strongest warrior

D. Supreme military general

235. What were the public meeting places during the Enlightenment called in England?

A. Salons

B. Forums

C. Coffeehouses

D. Agora

Answers

221. B. The Scientific Revolution
222. A. John Locke
223. A. Because it was a time when science and logic were used to solve social problems
224. A. John Locke
225. B. France
226. D. All of the above
227. D. All of the above
228. B. Adam Smith
229. C. Thomas Hobbes
230. D. All of the above
231. D. Emancipation of slaves
232. C. Edward Gibbon
233. A. John Stuart Mill
234. B. All-powerful ruler
235. C. Coffeehouses

The Glorious Revolution in England (1688–1689)

The Glorious Revolution of 1688-1689 was a notable event in England's history. King James II was replaced by his daughter Mary and her husband William, who were invited to take the throne as joint rulers. This changed the balance of power between Parliament and the monarchy forever! The revolution also brought religious freedom to England, allowing people to practice their faith without fear of persecution or punishment.

236. What caused the Glorious Revolution in England?

A. A disagreement over taxes

B. Dissatisfaction with the monarchy

C. King James II's Catholic sympathies

D. All of the above

237. How did William and Mary become rulers during the Glorious Revolution?

A. By declaring war against England

B. They were elected by the people

C. King James appointed them as his successors

D. Through a series of deals with the nobility and the Parliament

238. What was the nationality of William of Orange?

A. English

B. Danish

C. Dutch

D. French

239. How did the Glorious Revolution affect English politics?

A. It gave more power to the nobles

B. It created an absolute monarchy

C. Parliament gained more power

D. None of the above

240. What was one result of the Glorious Revolution in England?

A. A decrease in religious violence

B. An increase in taxes

C. The end of freedom of religion

D. All of the above

241. What was the "Bill of Rights"?

A. A document that granted King James II more power

B. An agreement between William and Mary about how they would rule together

C. A list of rights for English citizens that limited the powers of kings and queens

D. None of the above

242. What religion did Mary, the daughter of King James II, follow?

A. Islam

B. Protestantism

C. Judaism

D. Catholicism

243. What happened to King James II after the Glorious Revolution?

A. He was executed for treason

B. He was reincorporated into English political life

C. He was forced to go into exile

D. None of the above

244. Who was the main political rival of William III in Europe?

    A. Louis XIV

    B. Louis XV

    C. Charles V

    D. William IV

245. How did the Glorious Revolution affect English citizens?

    A. It gave them greater religious freedoms

    B. It increased their taxes

    C. It weakened their civil liberties

    D. None of the above

Answers

236. D. All of the above
237. D. Through a series of deals with the nobility and the Parliament
238. C. Dutch
239. C. Parliament gained more power
240. A. a decrease in religious violence
241. C. A list of rights for English citizens that limited the powers of kings and queens
242. B. Protestantism
243. C. He was forced to go into exile
244. A. Louis XIV
245. A. It gave them greater religious freedoms

The Georgian Era in English History (1714–1837)

The Georgian period in English history was a time of notable change. During this era, the country experienced advances in science and technology, an expanding economy, and increased overseas exploration. The Georgians were also known for their love of fashion, art, and culture. This exciting time saw a blossoming of new ideas that helped shape Britain into the modern nation it is today!

246. The period of English history known as the Georgian era is named after which royal family?

A. House of York

B. House of Stuart

C. House of Windsor

D. House of Hanover

247. What event marked the end of the Georgian era in England?

A. Industrial Revolution

B. Great Fire of London

C. Battle of Waterloo

D. Accession of Queen Victoria to the throne

248. Which important legal document was adopted in the 1830s by the Georgian rulers of England?

A. Bill of Rights

B. Magna Carta

C. Royal Proclamation

D. Slavery Abolition Act

249. What was the official religion of England during the Georgian era?

A. Protestantism

B. Catholicism

C. Atheism

D. Anglicanism

250. Who founded the British Museum, an institution that still stands today?

A. Prince Albert

B. William Pitt

C. Lord Liverpool

D. Sir Hans Sloane

251. Which was the major political rival of Great Britain during this time?

A. France

B. Sweden

C. Austria

D. Russia

252. Which of these important developments originated during the Georgian era?

A. Colonization

B. Industrialization

C. Imperialism

D. None of the above

253. Which Protestant denomination gained a lot of following during this period?

A. Baptist Church

B. Evangelicalism

C. Presbyterianism

D. Puritanism

254. Who was the first prime minister of England during the Georgian era?

A. William Pitt

B. Lord North

C. Robert Walpole

D. Charles Grey

255. Which economic policy became popular in Britain during the Georgian era?

A. Capitalism

B. Socialism

C. Mercantilism

D. Communism

256. Which Scottish thinker is the author of *A Treatise of Human Nature*?

A. David Hume

B. John Locke

C. John Milton

D. Adam Ferguson

257. Under which king did England lose control of the Thirteen Colonies?

A. George IV

B. George V

C. George VI

D. George III

258. Who wrote *Gulliver's Travels*, one of the most popular works from the Georgian era?

A. Jonathan Swift

B. Jane Austen

C. Charles Dickens

D. Robert Burns

259. Which of these statements is true about the Georgian period in English history?

A. The Georgian era was relatively unimportant in English history

B. The Georgian era was marked by great social upheaval that destabilized the nation for generations

C. The Georgian era was instrumental in helping Great Britain become a global power

D. The Georgian era is considered the Golden Age of British history

260. What was an important economic factor during this period in English history?

A. Expansion of trade

B. Introduction of capitalism

C. Increase in French tariffs

D. Social welfare policies

261. Which architectural style became popular among wealthy citizens during the Georgian era?

A. Baroque

B. Gothic

C. Neoclassical

D. Victorian

262. Which of these conflicts were not fought during the Georgian era?

A. Seven Years' War

B. Thirty Years' War

C. Napoleonic Wars

D. American Revolutionary War

263. Which famous book, which is still widely read today, was published in England during the Georgian era?

A. *Frankenstein*

B. *Wuthering Heights*

C. *Pride and Prejudice*

D. *Robinson Crusoe*

264. Which playwright wrote *The School for Scandal,* a popular theatrical production of the era?

A. William Shakespeare

B. George Bernard Shaw

C. John Gay

D. Richard Brinsley Sheridan

265. Which important economic document was agreed upon by Great Britain during the Georgian era?

A. Common Market Agreement

B. Bretton Woods Agreement

C. Magna Carta

D. Navigation Acts

Answers

246. D. House of Hanover
247. D. Accession of Queen Victoria to the throne
248. D. Slavery Abolition Act
249. D. Anglicanism
250. D. Sir Hans Sloane
251. A. France
252. B. Industrialization
253. B. Evangelicalism
254. C. Robert Walpole
255. C. Mercantilism
256. A. David Hume
257. D. George III
258. A. Jonathan Swift
259. C. The Georgian era was instrumental in helping Great Britain become a global power
260. A. Expansion of trade
261. C. Neoclassical
262. B. Thirty Years' War
263. D. *Robinson Crusoe*
264. D. Richard Brinsley Sheridan
265. D. Navigation Acts

Industrial Revolution in English History (1760–1840)

The Industrial Revolution was a period of notable change in English history from 1760 to 1840. During this time, new inventions and ideas transformed how people worked and lived. Machines replaced manual labor, allowing production levels to skyrocket. Factories were built across England. People moved to cities for work opportunities, and wealth grew rapidly. This exciting time changed our lives forever. Who knew what amazing things would come next?

266. What is considered the main catalyst behind the Industrial Revolution?

   A. Technological inventions that accelerated the rate of production

   B. Policies of the British government after the loss of the Thirteen Colonies

   C. Peace agreement between Britain and France in 1815

   D. Building canals and expanding trade networks

267. During what century did most countries experience their Industrial Revolution?

   A. Eighteenth century

   B. Nineteenth century

   C. Twentieth century

   D. Twenty-first century

268. Which of these figures is considered instrumental in the development of the spinning frame?

A. William Wilberforce

B. Adam Smith

C. Richard Arkwright

D. Robert Owen

269. What type of industry experienced the greatest increase in production during the Industrial Revolution?

A. Textiles

B. Iron and Steel

C. Mining

D. Automotive

270. Which of these figures is credited with the invention of the steam engine?

A. Robert Owen

B. James Watt

C. Edmund Cartwright

D. None of the above

271. What was one result of industrialization in England?

A. Increased poverty of the masses

B. Overthrow of the monarchy

C. No major change

D. Increased production and wealth

272. How did new transportation improvements help cause the Industrial Revolution?

A. By increasing access to resources

B. By creating more efficient shipping routes

C. By making it easier for workers to travel

D. All of the above

273. Which instrument is not typically credited with increasing productivity during the Industrial Revolution?

A. Spinning wheel

B. Steam engine

C. Power loom

D. Printing press

274. Which of these was not an immediate negative effect of the Industrial Revolution?

A. Decreased wages

B. Increased class disparity

C. Environmental damage

D. More job opportunities

275. The problems created by the Industrial Revolution would be criticized by which major thinker of the nineteenth century?

A. John Stuart Mill

B. Abraham Lincoln

C. Karl Marx

D. Friedrich Hegel

276. What type of organization emerged during the Industrial Revolution that allowed skilled workers to negotiate with employers and achieve higher wages?

A. Labor unions

B. Guilds

C. Corporations

D. None of the above

277. What invention managed to regulate the speed of the steam engine that ultimately increased production?

A. Railways

B. Coal chute

C. Spinning jennies

D. Watt's governor

278. Which of these was not an effect of the Industrial Revolution?

A. A decrease in England's population

B. Expansion of the kingdom's colonial holdings

C. Rise of workers' rights movements

D. An increase in overall trade

279. How did new inventions such as spinning jennies and power looms revolutionize the textile industry?

A. Allowed for mass production

B. Increased labor costs

C. Reduced quality of the products

D. None of the above

280. What major occurrence preceded the Industrial Revolution and was important in bringing it about?

A. The Bill of Rights

B. Increase in Britain's agricultural production

C. The end of the Napoleonic Wars

D. None of the above

281. What was the effect of the Industrial Revolution on demographic patterns?

A. More people started to emigrate to Asia

B. Increased national mortality rate

C. Large-scale urban growth

D. All of the above

282. Who is credited with the invention of the spinning jenny?

A. Lewis Paul

B. James Watt

C. Daniel Bourn

D. James Hargreaves

283. When was the spinning jenny invented?

A. 1760

B. 1764

C. 1768

D. 1772

284. What energy source was used increasingly during this period, allowing for improved steam engine efficiency?

A. Water power

B. Petroleum

C. Coal

D. Solar power

285. What did the Reform Act of 1832 do?

A. Increase wages

B. Create a democracy

C. End slavery

D. Expand voting rights

Answers

266. A. Technological inventions that accelerated the rate of production
267. B. Nineteenth century
268. C. Richard Arkwright
269. A. Textiles
270. B. James Watt
271. D. Increased production and wealth
272. D. All of the above
273. D. Printing press
274. C. Environmental damage
275. C. Karl Marx
276. A. Labor unions
277. D. Watt's governor
278. A. A decrease in England's population
279. A. Allowed for mass production
280. B. Increase in Britain's agricultural production
281. C. Large-scale urban growth
282. D. James Hargreaves
283. B. 1764
284. C. Coal
285. D. Expand voting rights

Victorian Era (1837–1901)

Welcome to the Victorian Era, an exciting time in history! This period, which stretched from 1837 to 1901, was named after Queen Victoria. During this time, new inventions were created, including the telephone, typewriter, and light bulb. People also traveled around the world more than ever before. Explorers discovered new lands filled with exotic plants and animals. Fashion changed drastically during this era as well. Men wore suits with top hats, while women dressed in big hoop skirts over multiple layers of petticoats!

286. What type of government did England have during the Victorian era?

   A. A constitutional monarchy

   B. A socialist state

   C. An absolute monarchy

   D. A democratic republic

287. When did the Great Exhibition take place in London, England?

   A. 1851

   B. 1900

   C. 1837

   D. 1901

288. What invention made transportation easier and faster for people during this period?

A. Airplanes

B. Automobile

C. Trains

D. Hot air balloons

289. When did Queen Victoria succeed the throne?

A. 1870

B. 1873

C. 1875

D. 1877

290. What caused a rise in industrialization during the Victorian era?

A. Increased trade with foreign countries

B. Expansion of transportation networks

C. Development of new technologies

D. All of the above

291. How did Queen Victoria's husband, Prince Albert, die?

A. He was assassinated

B. Natural causes

C. In an accident

D. From an illness

292. When was the Act of Union with Ireland established?

A. January 1, 1801

B. March 1, 1800

C. December 25, 1802

D. None of the above

293. What significant social reform occurred during the Victorian era?

A. Legalization of abortion

B. Abolition of slavery

C. Women's suffrage

D. Prohibition of alcohol

294. How did Queen Victoria react to her husband's death?

A. It did not have an effect on her

B. She refused to leave the castle

C. She wore black for the rest of her life

D. She abdicated

295. What was the main religion in England during this period?

A. Presbyterianism

B. Buddhism

C. Roman Catholicism

D. Anglicanism

296. When was the East India Company dissolved?

A. 1850

B. 1857

C. 1869

D. 1874

297. How can Britain's foreign policy direction during the Victorian era be best summarized?

A. It remained largely the same

B. It became more aggressive

C. It was focused on the containment of the United States

D. It was the biggest failure of the Victorian era

298. When was Lord William Salisbury first elected to the office of prime minister?

A. 1880

B. 1885

C. 1887

D. 1895

299. Which royal house did Queen Victoria belong to?

A. Stuart

B. Windsor

C. Hanover

D. Habsburg

300. To whom was Queen Victoria's eldest daughter, Victoria, married?

A. Kaiser Frederick II

B. Kaiser Wilhelm II

C. Tsar Nicholas

D. None of the above

301. When did Queen Victoria celebrate her Golden Jubilee?

A. 1887

B. 1877

C. 1867

D. 1897

302. What did the "Diamond Jubilee" mark?

A. Half a century of Victoria's rule

B. Sixty years of Victoria's rule

C. Celebration of the Glorious Revolution

D. None of the above

303. Who was the grandfather of Queen Victoria?

A. George III

B. Prince Edward

C. Charles II

D. James VII and II

304. Who succeeded Queen Victoria as king of the United Kingdom?

A. George IV

B. Charles III

C. Edward VII

D. James VIII

305. How was Queen Victoria referred to, during her lifetime and afterward, because of her successful and international reign?

A. The Iron Lady

B. The Supreme Queen

C. The Grandmother of Europe

D. The Arbiter of Europe

Answers

286. A. A constitutional monarchy
287. A. 1851
288. C. Trains
289. B. 1873
290. D. All of the above
291. D. From an illness
292. A. January 1, 1801
293. B. Abolition of slavery
294. C. She wore black for the rest of her life
295. D. Anglicanism
296. D. 1874
297. B. It became more aggressive
298. B. 1885
299. C. Hanover
300. A. Kaiser Frederick II
301. A. 1887
302. B. sixty years of Victoria's rule
303. A. George III
304. C. Edward VII
305. C. The Grandmother of Europe

The Boer Wars and England in South Africa (1899–1902)

The United Kingdom waged two wars against the local Boer population of South Africa during the reign of Queen Victoria. It was a long and difficult conflict that lasted for many years. The British troops faced fierce resistance from the Boer forces in battles fought across the country. As more soldiers were sent from England, new strategies were introduced to try to win the war, but victory was not easy!

306. Who was fighting in the Boer War?

    A. France and Germany

    B. England and South Africa

    C. England and Scotland

    D. United States and Mexico

307. Why was there a war between Britain and South Africa?

    A. For freedom of religion

    B. To gain control over mineral resources

    C. To spread European culture

    D. Over conflicting political beliefs

308. When did the First Boer War begin?

    A. 1878

    B. 1880

    C. 1882

    D. 1884

309. Which British politician was responsible for annexing South African territories for the British in 1877?

A. Winston Churchill

B. Lord Salisbury

C. Sir Theophilus Shepstone

D. Robert Baden-Powell

310. Who declared a state of rebellion in 1899, leading to the Boer War?

A. Cecil Rhodes

B. Queen Victoria

C. Paul Kruger

D. Robert Baden-Powell

311. What type of government ruled South Africa at the time of the Boer War?

A. Republic

B. Monarchy

C. Dictatorship

D. Democracy

312. Who were known as "Boers" in South Africa during the Boer War?

A. African tribesmen

B. British settlers

C. Dutch colonists

D. French refugees

313. What was agreed upon in the peace agreement after the First Boer War?

A. British rights to South African minerals

B. Different degrees of citizenship for Boers and British

C. Dissolution of the South African Republic

D. Self-governance for the Boers under British protection

314. When did the Second Boer War break out?

   A. 1889

   B. 1890

   C. 1899

   D. 1900

315. How many military casualties did the British suffer during the Boer War?

   A. 90,000

   B. 150,000

   C. 250,000

   D. 350,000

316. Approximately how many civilians were affected by the Second Boer War?

   A. 50,000

   B. 90,000

   C. 130,000

   D. 170,000

317. What does the word "Boer" mean?

   A. Inhabitant

   B. Traveler

   C. Colonist

   D. Farmer

318. Who became one of the leaders of the British Army in early 1900 and swung the tide for the British?

   A. Winston Churchill

   B. Robert Baden-Powell

   C. Lord Kitchener

   D. Douglas Haig

319. Which treaty ended the Second Boer War?

   A. Treaty of Amsterdam

   B. Treaty of Cape Town

   C. Treaty of Williamsburg

   D. Treaty of Vereeniging

320. What was the result of the Boer Wars?

    A. British victory

    B. South African independence

    C. Stalemate

    D. None of the above

Answers

306. B. England and South Africa
307. B. To gain control over mineral resources
308. B. 1880
309. C. Sir Theophilus Shepstone
310. C. Paul Kruger
311. A. Republic
312. C. Dutch colonists
313. D. Self-governance of the Boers under British protection
314. C. 1899
315. A. 90,000
316. A. 50,000
317. D. Farmer
318. C. Lord Kitchener
319. D. Treaty of Vereeniging
320. A. British victory

The Edwardian Era (1901–1914)

The Edwardian era was a time of significant change in England from 1901 to 1914. During this period, King Edward VII ruled the country and made many improvements. He brought new technology and ideas that revolutionized transportation, communication, entertainment, fashion—you name it! People had more freedom to travel around the world than ever before. There were exciting new inventions, like cars and airplanes, that changed how people got around. Life during this era was fast-paced and full of fun.

321. What major advancement in the field of transport coincided with the Edwardian era?

    A. Invention of railways

    B. Invention of commercial aircrafts

    C. Invention of automobiles

    D. All of the above

322. When did Edward VII ascend the throne?

    A. 1901

    B. 1911

    C. 1902

    D. 1903

323. Whose son was Edward VII?

A. Edward VI's

B. Charles III's

C. Queen Victoria's

D. George V's

324. Who founded The National Trust during this period?

A. Charles Darwin

B. Winston Churchill

C. John Ruskin

D. Alfred Nobel

325. How old was Edward VII when he became king?

A. 38

B. 49

C. 54

D. 60

326. Under Edward VII, major reforms were passed in which areas of British life?

A. Industry

B. Social welfare

C. Military

D. Working conditions

327. Which power was the main rival of Great Britain during this time?

A. France

B. Russia

C. Germany

D. None of the above

328. Why are the years 1909-1910 considered the most challenging years of Edward VII's life?

A. Because of the death of his second-born son

B. Because of the ongoing constitutional crisis

C. Because of the outbreak of World War I

D. Because of the economic problems created overseas

329. Who was the prime minister of Great Britain from 1902 to 1905?

A. Archibald Primrose

B. J.M Barrie

C. Arthur Balfour

D. H. H. Asquith

330. Which political party pushed for impressive reforms during the Edwardian era?

A. The Liberal Party

B. The Conservative Party

C. The Whigs

D. None of the above

331. When was the Labour Party founded?

A. 1848

B. 1900

C. 1910

D. None of the above

332. When did Edward VII die?

A. 1909

B. 1910

C. 1911

D. 1912

333. How did industry expand during this time?

A. Steel production increased

B. New technologies changed working conditions

C. Factories opened around Europe

D. All of the above

334. Who succeeded Edward VII as king?

A. Edward VIII

B. George V

C. Charles III

D. Henry IX

335. Which of these statements best describes the domestic situation in Great Britain during the Edwardian era?

A. Great Britain was able to cement its power as a global hegemon

B. Domestic politics were relatively stable and progress-oriented

C. Britain's prime ministers proceeded to break with the will of the monarchy

D. None of the above

Answers

321. C. Invention of automobiles
322. A. 1901
323. C. Queen Victoria's
324. C. John Ruskin
325. D. 60
326. C. Military
327. C. Germany
328. B. Because of the ongoing constitutional crisis
329. C. Arthur Balfour
330. A. The Liberal Party
331. B. 1900
332. B. 1910
333. D. All of the above
334. B. George V
335. B. Domestic politics were relatively stable and progress-oriented

World War I in English History (1914–1918)

World War I was a notable event in English history, beginning in 1914 and ending in 1918. Young men from England were sent to fight in battles across Europe as they sought to protect their homeland. As the war raged on, those at home faced shortages of food and fuel while dealing with the fear of losing loved ones overseas. The brave individuals who fought for their country helped shape our lives today, making World War I an unforgettable part of English history.

336. Who was the leader of England during World War I?

    A. King George V

    B. Queen Victoria

    C. Prime Minister David Lloyd George

    D. Winston Churchill

337. Why did England formally enter WWI?

    A. To increase its power and land holdings

    B. To help Germany win the war

    C. To protect Belgium from German invasion

    D. To prevent further spread of Communism

338. How long did World War I last in Europe?

    A. Two years

    B. Four years

    C. Six months

    D. Ten years

339. What was the main cause of WWI?

    A. Unification of Europe

    B. Industrial Revolution

    C. Militarism and alliances

    D. Spread of Communism

340. Which nations constituted the Entente in WWI, outside of Britain?

    A. Germany, Austria-Hungary, and Turkey

    B. France, Russia, and the United States

    C. France and Italy

    D. Serbia, Bulgaria, and Japan

341. Who were known as the "Lost Generation"?

    A. Soldiers who survived World War I

    B. Civilians who fought in World War I

    C. Artists, writers, and intellectuals affected by WWI

    D. Women involved in war efforts

342. Who was the British prime minister at the time of the outbreak of the war?

    A. Winston Churchill

    B. H. H. Asquith

    C. David Lloyd George

    D. Arthur Balfour

343. In which of these battles did Britain achieve decisive victories?

    A. Battle of the Somme

    B. Battle of Verdun

    C. First Battle of Ypres

    D. None of the above

344. The leader of which major European superpower that took part in the war was a first cousin of **Britain's** George V?

A. France

B. Austria

C. Russia

D. Prussia

345. When was the Defense of the Realm Act (DORA) passed, giving government an **increased** range of competences during the war?

A. 1914

B. 1915

C. 1916

D. 1917

Answers

336. A. King George V
337. C. To protect Belgium from German invasion
338. B. Four years
339. C. Militarism and alliances
340. B. France, Russia, and the United States
341. C. Artists, writers, and intellectuals affected by WWI
342. B. H. H. Asquith
343. D. None of the above
344. C. Russia
345. A. 1914

Interwar Britain (1918–1939)

Between 1918 and 1939, Great Britain experienced a period of transformation. After World War I ended in 1918, people were eager to put the horrors of war behind them and move on with their lives. Technological advances brought new industries, and improved transportation systems connected cities throughout the country like never before. Although there were hardships during this time known as interwar Britain, it was also a period filled with creativity, progress, and optimism for what could come next!

346. What was the name of the British prime minister from 1937 to 1940?

    A. Neville Chamberlain

    B. Winston Churchill

    C. Stanley Baldwin

    D. Clement Attlee

347. In what year did women first get the right to vote in Britain?

    A. 1918

    B. 1928

    C. 1938

    D. 1935

348. How many countries were part of the League of Nations when it formed in 1920?

A. 10

B. 23

C. 20

D. 42

349. Which European power was forced to pay massive war reparations according to the Treaty of Versailles?

A. Germany

B. France

C. Italy

D. Austria

350. What was the principal declared objective of the League of Nations?

A. To contain the rise of Germany

B. To stop the spread of Communism

C. To maintain world peace

D. All of the above

351. What was the name of the British Empire's first battle cruiser, built in 1907?

A. HMS *Dreadnaught*

B. HMS *Eagle*

C. HMS *Argus*

D. HMS *Invincible*

352. Which political party gained power in 1924 after winning a landslide victory?

A. Labour Party

B. Conservative Party

C. Liberal Party

D. Communist Party

353. In what year did Britain and Ireland sign the Anglo-Irish Treaty, effectively forming the Irish Free State?

A. 1919

B. 1921

C. 1928

D. 1931

354. Who was the first woman elected to Parliament in Britain?

A. Nancy Astor

B. Emmeline Pankhurst

C. Margaret Thatcher

D. Tiffany Brooks

355. What event caused economic depression and high unemployment rates throughout 1930s Britain?

A. The Wall Street Crash

B. Formation of the Soviet Union

C. Prohibition

D. Industrial Revolution

356. Where were the peace talks held between the participants of WWI?

A. Berlin

B. London

C. Washington

D. Paris

357. About how many British soldiers died in WWI?

A. 3,000,000

B. 6,000,000

C. 800,000

D. 1,300,000

358. Who wrote *The Road to Wigan Pier*, a book about working class life in interwar Britain?

A. J.R.R. Tolkien

B. George Orwell

C. Virginia Woolf

D. H.G. Wells

359. In what year did unemployment peak under Prime Minister Ramsay MacDonald's government?

A. 1929

B. 1932

C. 1935

D. 1938

360. Which party formed the government in Britain in 1924?

A. Conservatives

B. Labour

C. Liberals

D. Whigs

361. Which new state did Britain recognize in early February of 1924?

A. Empire of Japan

B. German Federal Republic

C. Soviet Union

D. Yugoslavia

362. In what year was the Citizens Advice Bureau founded by a group of charities, lawyers, and social reformers?

A. 1939

B. 1925

C. 1929

D. 1935

363. The rule of which British monarch was subject to a constitutional crisis in 1936?

A. George V

B. Edward VII

C. George VI

D. Edward VIII

364. When did the British government launch a national rearmament program, following similar efforts from Nazi Germany?

A. 1933

B. 1934

C. 1935

D. 1936

365. In what year did King George V make his first royal Christmas broadcast to the British people?

    A. 1925

    B. 1932

    C. 1935

    D. 1940

Answers

346. A. Neville Chamberlain
347. A. 1918
348. D. 42
349. A. Germany
350. C. To maintain world peace
351. D. HMS *Invincible*
352. B. Conservative Party
353. B. 1921
354. A. Nancy Astor
355. A. The Wall Street Crash
356. D. Paris
357. C. 800,000
358. B. George Orwell
359. C. 1935
360. B. Labour
361. C. Soviet Union
362. A. 1939
363. D. Edward VIII
364. B. 1934
365. B. 1932

The General Strike in England (1926)

In 1926, England experienced a big event called the General Strike. It was when millions of workers went on strike to protest unfair working conditions and wages. For nine days, large parts of the country stopped running as people all over showed their support for the cause. This historic moment changed Britain forever!

366. How long did the General Strike of 1926 last?

A. Two days

B. Ten weeks

C. Four months

D. Nine days

367. Who called for the General Strike?

A. The British Army

B. Trade unions

C. The Labour Party

D. Prime minister

368. Why was the strike held?

A. To protest reduced wages

B. To end the rule of the Conservative government

C. To promote democracy

D. None of the above

369. Which group of workers were concerned the most with the strike?

    A. Doctors and nurses

    B. Steel workers

    C. Lawyers

    D. Coal miners

370. What was the result of the General Strike?

    A. The government was changed

    B. The strike was called off after a stalemate

    C. Employers gave higher wages to their workforce

    D. None of the above

371. What was the average wage for miners by the time of the strike?

    A. Three pounds

    B. Six pounds

    C. Eight pounds

    D. Nine pounds

372. When did the strike begin?

    A. May 1

    B. May 4

    C. May 10

    D. May 15

373. About how many people participated in the strike?

    A. Ten million

    B. Two million

    C. Five million

    D. Eight hundred thousand

374. Which of these statements is true about the economic situation of post-WWI Britain?

    A. Britain was the richest nation on earth

    B. Britain had a relatively stable economy

    C. Britain suffered the most from the 1929 Great Depression

    D. None of the above

375. Which of these was not among the demands of the workers during the 1926 General Strike?

A. Increasing the cost of living

B. Increasing the wages

C. Decreasing working hours

D. Granting more rights to trade unions

Answers

366. D. Nine days
367. B. Trade unions
368. A. To protest reduced wages
369. D. Coal miners
370. B. The strike was called off after a stalemate
371. A. Three pounds
372. B. May 4
373. B. Two million
374. B. Britain had a relatively stable economy
375. A. Increasing the cost of living

The Great Depression in England (1929–1939)

The Great Depression was a difficult time for England between 1929 and 1939. Many people struggled to put food on the table, others couldn't find jobs, and some even lost their homes. It was an incredibly tough period in history that made life hard for families nationwide. People had to get creative and work together to survive these trying times.

376. What event began the Great Depression in England?

    A. The Wall Street Crash of 1929

    B. World War I

    C. The rise of Nazi Germany

    D. The influenza pandemic

377. Which English prime minister helped introduce social welfare during the Great Depression?

    A. Winston Churchill

    B. David Lloyd George

    C. Neville Chamberlain

    D. Clement Attlee

378. Which statement is true about unemployment levels in Britain during this period?

    A. They remained mostly steady

    B. They increased by a noticeable amount

    C. They drastically decreased

    D. None of the above

379. Which of these areas was hit the hardest with economic problems caused by the Great Depression?

    A. London

    B. Dover

    C. Birmingham

    D. None of the above

380. How did disruptions in trade affect England's economy during the Great Depression?

    A. It created more competition from other countries

    B. It encouraged global economic growth

    C. It resulted in lower prices and increased exports

    D. It contributed to the rise of unemployment

381. Why do historians consider the destructive results of the Great Depression in Britain relatively modest?

    A. Because of the staunch policies of the government

    B. Because of the charities set up by the monarchy

    C. Because of the already strong economy it had

    D. Because of the recession it had already been experiencing before 1929

382. When did the British government switch back to the gold standard after WWI?

    A. 1921

    B. 1925

    C. 1929

    D. 1933

383. When did Britain begin to recover from the Great Depression?

A. 1930

B. 1933

C. 1939

D. 1940

384. What was only way people were able to cope economically with the effects of the Great Depression?

A. By gambling

B. By relying on charitable donations

C. By spending less and saving more

D. None of the above

385. How did the Great Depression in England end?

A. With a new economic stimulus plan

B. With the introduction of rationing

C. With military victory against Germany

D. With an increase in global trade

Answers

376. A. The Wall Street Crash of 1929
377. B. David Lloyd George
378. B. They increased by a noticeable amount
379. C. Birmingham
380. D. It contributed to the rise of unemployment
381. D. Because of the recession it had been experiencing before 1929
382. B. 1925
383. B. 1933
384. C. By spending less and saving more
385. C. With military victory against Germany

England's Involvement in World War II (1939–1945)

When World War II broke out in 1939, England was one of the first countries to join the fight. For six long years, brave British people worked together to protect their country and stand up for freedom globally. They faced many challenges along the way as they fought against Nazi forces. But despite all odds, England persevered and helped bring about a victorious end to WWII!

386. Who was England's leader during WWII?

    A. Winston Churchill

    B. Queen Elizabeth II

    C. Adolf Hitler

    D. Franklin Roosevelt

387. When did Germany invade Poland, causing Britain to declare war on them?

    A. June 8, 1938

    B. September 1, 1939

    C. December 5, 1941

    D. April 15, 1945

388. In what year did Japan attack Pearl Harbor, bringing America into the war as an ally of Britain and other Allied countries?

A. May 9, 1941

B. December 8, 1941

C. June 22, 1942

D. April 28, 1945

389. On which war theater were British forces most concentrated throughout the war?

A. The Pacific Theater

B. The Eastern Front

C. The Western Front

D. The North African Theater

390. Who were Britain's main allies during World War II?

A. Germany, Japan, and Italy

B. France, the US, and the USSR

C. France, Germany, and Spain

D. None of the above

Answers

386. A. Winston Churchill
387. B. September 1,1939
388. B. December 8,1941
389. C. The Western Front
390. B. France, the US, and the USSR

The Blitz (1940–1941)

years, the British people demonstrated extraordinary courage and resilience, especially during the Blitz—a relentless bombing campaign by German forces from 1940 to 1941. Cities were shattered, lives disrupted, yet the spirit of unity and defiance never wavered. Against overwhelming odds, Britain stood firm, playing a vital role in the Allied victory and the global fight for freedom.

391. What was the goal of the Blitz?

    A. To conquer England

    B. To destroy military targets

    C. To demoralize civilians

    D. All of the above

392. Why were people evacuated from their homes during the Blitz?

    A. To keep them safe from bombings

    B. To make room for German soldiers

    C. To provide them with better living conditions

    D. To find work in other cities

393. From which word does the word "Blitz" originate?

    A. Blitzcrank

    B. Blitzkrieg

    C. Blitzortung

    D. None of the above

394. How did the British people respond to the Blitz?

    A. They surrendered to German forces

    B. They fled their homes

    C. They fought back with military force

    D. They stayed in their homes and endured

395. When did the bombing of London begin?

    A. September 1, 1940

    B. September 7, 1940

    C. September 21, 1940

    D. September 26, 1940

396. When did the Battle of Britain begin?

    A. July 1940

    B. February 1941

    C. October 1940

    D. December 1940

397. Who oversaw planning the attacks on Britain during the Blitz?

    A. Adolf Hitler

    B. Joseph Goebbels

    C. Joseph Stalin

    D. Hermann Goering

398. What was used as an effective bomb shelter against the Germans by the population of London?

    A. Tower Bridge

    B. London Underground

    C. Westminster Abbey

    D. All of the above

399. Who won the Battle of Britain?

    A. Great Britain

    B. Nazi Germany

    C. Soviet Union

    D. It was a draw

400. How many British casualties were caused by the Blitz?

    A. 10,000–20,000

    B. 50,000–60,000

    C. 100,000–150,000

    D. 200,000–300,000

Answers

391. D. All of the above
392. A. To keep them safe from bombings
393. B. Blitzkrieg
394. D. They stayed in their homes and endured
395. B. September 7, 1940
396. A. July 1940
397. D. Hermann Goering
398. B. London Underground
399. A. Great Britain
400. C. 100,000–150,000

The Cold War in Relation to England (1947–1991)

England was part of the Cold War from 1947 to 1991. This war was between two competing superpowers, the United States and Russia. It was a time of tension, distrust, and fear as both sides built up weapons to gain power over each other. England played a significant role during this period as it provided support for one side against the other. The Cold War had a notable impact on people's lives all around the world!

401. What was the purpose of the talks held by the victorious nations in WWII?

    A. To stop Communism from spreading

    B. To protect democratic governments

    C. To create a new world order

    D. All of the above

402. How did Britain respond to Soviet aggression during the Cold War?

    A. With military action

    B. By allying with the United States

    C. By strengthening its economy

    D. It didn't respond

403. After WWII, what was the main measure Britain resorted to for protection from a potential Soviet threat during the Cold War?

A. It formed a nuclear arsenal

B. It developed stronger ties with France

C. It increased trade restrictions on Russia

D. It decreased social spending

404. During which of the following events did the Cold War reach its peak?

A. The Cuban Missile Crisis

B. The collapse of the Soviet Union

C. The fall of Communism

D. The rise of nuclear weapons

405. How did Britain react to the dissolution of the Soviet Union in 1991?

A. It took part in efforts to build up Russia

B. It increased military expenditure

C. It withdrew from NATO

D. It reduced its international presence

406. What was one outcome of Britain's involvement in the Cold War?

A. An increase in global trade

B. An end to poverty across Europe

C. Heightened tensions between East and West

D. Improved relations with former enemies

407. Why is Winston's Churchill's speech in March 1946 considered important in this context?

A. It is considered the exact beginning of the Cold War

B. It presented the US and the UK as the defenders of a new world order

C. It heavily criticized the actions of the US government during WWII

D. It wished for a dissolution of the Soviet Union

408. What was one major consequence of increased tensions between East and West during the Cold War?

    A. The development of new weapons technologies

    B. Increased global trade

    C. Increased economic prosperity in Europe

    D. The rise of global Communism

409. What metaphor did Winston Churchill use to describe the political and ideological isolation of the USSR and the Communist states from the rest of the world in his 1946 speech?

    A. Iron Man

    B. Iron Wall

    C. Iron Curtain

    D. Iron Window

410. When did the Berlin Wall come down?

    A. 1941

    B. 1947

    C. 1989

    D. 1991

411. Which German territory did the British control after the Allied occupation following WWII?

    A. Northeast

    B. Northwest

    C. Southeast

    D. Southwest

412. How did Britain's involvement in the Cold War ultimately affect Europe?

    A. It led to stronger military capabilities in the West

    B. It improved economic prosperity across Europe

    C. It caused an arms race among nations

    D. All of the above

413. What was one consequence of the Cuban Missile Crisis?

   A. Increased military spending by Britain

   B. The dissolution of NATO

   C. Improved relations with former Communist states

   D. Heightened tensions between the USSR and the US

414. Which of the following is true about the military involvement of Britain during the conflicts of the Cold War?

   A. Britain was never involved in military conflicts during the Cold War

   B. Britain's involvement in military conflicts during the Cold War was minimal

   C. Britain was actively involved in military conflicts during the Cold War

   D. Britain exclusively pledged economic support for military conflicts during the Cold War

415. What was the result of the elections held in the UK after WWII?

   A. Conservative victory

   B. Liberal Party was victorious

   C. Labour Party gained power

   D. None of the above

416. What was a major consequence for the British Empire after WWII?

   A. Britain was forced to give up all claims to its colonial territories immediately

   B. Britain has kept its overseas territories after WWII

   C. Britain had to gradually decolonize

   D. None of the above

417. What was "The Troubles"?

   A. An ethno-nationalist conflict in Ireland

   B. A period of austerity under the Labour government

   C. A three-year economic crisis

   D. None of the above

418. When did the UK become part of the European Union?

    A. 1970

    B. 1973

    C. 1975

    D. 1977

419. How did the Cold War end?

    A. With the signing of the Treaty of Paris

    B. With military action from both sides

    C. With an agreement between East and West Germany

    D. With the dissolution of Soviet Union

420. Which decade can be considered the most prosperous in Britain after WWII?

    A. 1990s

    B. 1980s

    C. 1970s

    D. 1950s

Answers

401. D. All of the above

402. B. By allying with the United States

403. A. It formed a nuclear arsenal

404. A. The Cuban Missile Crisis

405. A. It took part in efforts to build up Russia

406. D. Improved relations with former enemies

407. B. It presented the US and the UK as the defenders of a new world order

408. A. The development of new weapons technologies

409. C. Iron Curtain

410. C. 1989

411. B. Northwest

412. D. All of the above

413. D. Heightened tensions between the USSR and the US

414. C. Britain was actively involved in military conflicts during the Cold War

415. C. Labour Party gained power

416. C. Britain had to gradually decolonize

417. A. An ethno-nationalist conflict in Ireland

418. B. 1973

419. D. With the dissolution of Soviet Union

420. D. 1950s

The Coronation of Queen Elizabeth II (1953)

On the June 2, 1953, Queen Elizabeth II was formally crowned. She had been queen since February 6 of that same year when her father, King George VI, died. Thousands of people globally gathered to watch the coronation and celebrate Queen Elizabeth's reign as Britain's new monarch. It was a magnificent event with music, pageantry, and grandeur rarely seen in history!

421. When did the coronation ceremony of Queen Elizabeth II take place?

    A. December 25, 1950

    B. June 2, 1953

    C. May 14, 1952

    D. September 21, 1955

422. What is known as "the traditional crown" of the British monarchy?

    A. The Crown Jewels

    B. The Imperial State Crown

    C. St. Edward's Crown

    D. Royal Sceptre

423. Where did Queen Elizabeth take her coronation oath?

    A. Westminster Abbey

    B. Buckingham Palace

    C. Windsor Castle

    D. Tower of London

424. How old was Queen Elizabeth when she took the throne in 1952?

    A. 21 years old

    B. 25 years old

    C. 26 years old

    D. 18 years old

425. Who designed Queen Elizabeth II's coronation gown?

    A. Norman Hartnell

    B. Michael Kors

    C. Vivienne Westwood

    D. Hans Wegner

Answers

421. B. June 2, 1953
422. C. St. Edward's Crown
423. A. Westminster Abbey
424. B. 25 years old
425. A. Norman Hartnell

Margaret Thatcher Era (1979–1990)

Margaret Thatcher was Britain's first female prime minister and served from 1979 to 1990. During her time in office, she earned the nickname "The Iron Lady" for her ambitious and determined leadership style. Her policies included privatizing government services and industries and reducing income inequality through a series of social reforms. She also worked to strengthen Britain's foreign policy by negotiating with notable allies globally. This period in British history is known as the Margaret Thatcher era—an era filled with bold decision-making that shaped modern Britain!

426. What did Mrs. Thatcher do to help revive Britain's economy in the 1980s?

   A. Introduced free healthcare for all citizens

   B. Lowered taxes across the country

   C. Nationalized many industries

   D. Increased government spending

427. What international event happened early in Mrs. Thatcher's time as prime minister?

   A. Communism fell in Eastern Europe

   B. The Falklands War

   C. Brexiteer movement began

   D. NATO was expelled from Western Europe

428. What nickname was given to Mrs. Thatcher's economic policies by her opponents?

A. Iron Lady

B. The Great Communicator

C. TINA (there is no alternative)

D. Thatcherism

429. What did Margaret Thatcher do to try to reduce the influence of trade unions?

A. Introduced strict laws to limit their power

B. Raised taxes on union members

C. Encouraged workers' rights

D. Nationalized all corporations

430. What was Mrs. Thatcher famous for saying about freedom and capitalism?

A. Socialism works best when given a chance

B. Freedom means taking control of your own destiny

C. Capitalism must be regulated by governments

D. There is no such thing as free markets

431. How did Mrs. Thatcher's economic policies effect industry in Britain during the 1980s?

A. She closed down many factories

B. Increased government spending on new businesses

C. Tax cuts made it more profitable to invest in industry

D. She nationalized all corporations

432. By what nickname is Margaret Thatcher known today?

A. The Iron Lady

B. The Communicator

C. The Arbiter of Europe

D. The Labour Nightmare

433. What did Margaret Thatcher do with regard to taxes during the 1980s?

A. Raised them for everyone

B. Lowered them for the higher classes

C. Introduced a flat rate tax system

D. Abolished income taxes altogether

434. How did Mrs. Thatcher's economic policies impact Britain's manufacturing sector?

A. They caused it to collapse completely

B. The sector was nationalized

C. It saw rapid growth as taxes were cut

D. She implemented strict regulations in the industry

435. What did Margaret Thatcher do to promote home ownership?

A. Nationalized all housing

B. Introduced the Right to Buy legislation

C. Encouraged private landlords

D. Lowered interest rates on mortgages

436. How did Mrs. Thatcher's economic policies impact unemployment levels during her time in office?

A. They increased significantly

B. They stayed the same

C. Tax cuts made it easier to find jobs

D. They were reduced

437. Which organization attempted to assassinate Margaret Thatcher in October of 1984?

A. ISIS

B. IRA

C. The Black Hands

D. The International

438. How were Mrs. Thatcher's economic policies received by the Labour Party?

A. They were welcomed

B. Criticized for being too extreme

C. Seen as an improvement compared to previous governments

D. Ignored completely

439. In which European city did Margaret Thatcher give a speech in which she opposed the idea of a federal Europe?

A. Bruges

B. Brussels

C. Paris

D. Madrid

440. Until when was Margaret Thatcher the prime minister?

A. 1989

B. 1990

C. 1991

D. 1992

Answers

426. B. Lowered taxes across the country

427. B. The Falklands War

428. D. Thatcherism

429. A. Introduced strict laws to limit their power

430. B. Freedom means taking control of your own destiny

431. C. Tax cuts made it more profitable to invest in industry

432. A. The Iron Lady

433. B. Lowered them for the higher classes

434. C. It saw rapid growth as taxes were cut

435. B. Introduced the Right to Buy legislation

436. D. They were reduced

437. B. IRA

438. B. Criticized for being too extreme

439. A. Bruges

440. B. 1990

The Miners' Strike (1984–1985)

The Miners' Strike of 1984 was the longest strike in British history. Miners from all over Britain went on a massive strike for one year, starting in 1984 and ending in 1985. They were fighting against their employers' plans to close some of their coal mines. It was cold outside, but the miners stayed determined to make sure their voices would be heard! Despite many hardships, it was an inspiring event that had repercussions across the country and around the world.

441. What triggered the Miners' Strike of 1984?

    A. The introduction of new technology by the mining companies

    B. A dispute over pay and job security

    C. The closure of several coal mines in Scotland

    D. An increase in fuel prices for miners

442. How long did the strike last?

    A. one week

    B. two months

    C. six months

    D. eleven months

443. Who was prime minister during this time?

    A. John Major

    B. Margaret Thatcher

    C. Tony Blair

    D. Gordon Brown

444. Who led the miners during this period?

A. Arthur Scargill

B. David Cameron

C. Harold Wilson

D. Ian MacGregor

445. How did the workers primarily protest?

A. Using armed violence

B. Mass demonstrations

C. Non-violent civil disobedience

D. None of the above

446. What were some of the consequences of the strike for communities?

A. Job losses

B. Increased unemployment

C. Closures in local businesses

D. All of the above

447. What did mining companies accuse Arthur Scargill and his union of doing during this period?

A. Prolonging violence

B. Destroying morale

C. Encouraging a militant approach

D. None of the above

448. What was the outcome of the strike?

A. It was ruled illegal

B. A pay raise and job security

C. A complete firing of the miners

D. Privatization of the coal industry in 1985

449. Where did one of the most violent clashes between police and protesters take place in June 1984?

A. Birmingham

B. London

C. Yorkshire

D. Orgreave

450. How much money was given to striking miners by the National Union of Mineworkers (NUM)?

A. £2 million

B. £5 million

C. £8 million

D. £10 million

Answers

441. B. A dispute over pay and job security
442. D. eleven months
443. B. Margaret Thatcher
444. A. Arthur Scargill
445. C. Non-violent civil disobedience
446. D. All of the above
447. C. Encouraging a militant approach
448. A. It was ruled illegal
449. D. Orgreave
450. C. £8 Million

The Good Friday Agreement (1998)

The Good Friday Agreement was signed by many people who wanted a better future for the country. This agreement helped end years of violence between different groups and allowed everyone to live side-by-side in peace. Everyone promised to respect each other's cultures, traditions, and beliefs so that all people could live free from fear or discrimination. With this new agreement came the hope that things would get better!

451. What is the Good Friday Agreement?

- A. A peace agreement signed in 1998 to end conflict between Ireland and Northern Ireland
- B. A law passed by British Parliament in 1989 outlawing discrimination against minorities
- C. An international treaty that ended a long-standing border dispute between two countries
- D. The document outlining the terms for Scotland's independence from England

452. Who were involved with signing the Good Friday Agreement?

    A. Representatives of the Irish Republican Army (IRA), loyalist paramilitary organizations, and representatives from Britain, Europe, and the US State Department

    B. Only representatives from Britain

    C. Only representatives from the Irish Republic

    D. The prime ministers of UK/Ireland

453. What were the main outcomes of the Good Friday Agreement?

    A. The end of sectarian violence in Northern Ireland

    B. The establishment of a government in which nationalists and unionists shared power

    C. The secession of Northern Island from the United Kingdom

    D. Recognition of Scotland's independence

454. Where was the Good Friday Agreement signed?

    A. London, England

    B. Belfast, Northern Ireland

    C. Dublin, Republic of Ireland

    D. Washington, D.C.

455. What is the legal name of the Good Friday Agreement?

    A. The Republic of Ireland Peace Treaty

    B. The Belfast Agreement

    C. The British Irish Intergovernmental Conference

    D. The Anglo-Irish Agreement

456. Who was a major negotiator for the Good Friday Agreement, earning him a Nobel Peace Prize?

    A. Former Prime Minister Tony Blair

    B. Former US President Bill Clinton

    C. Former First Minister of Northern Ireland David Trimble

    D. Sinn Féin leader Gerry Adams

457. When was the agreement signed?

    A. May 22, 1998

    B. April 25, 1998

    C. April 10, 1998

    D. May 19, 1998

458. What did British Prime Minister Tony Blair say about the Good Friday Agreement?

    A. It was an important step toward peace in Northern Ireland

    B. It was a mistake to sign the agreement

    C. The agreement would have no impact on life in Northern Ireland

    D. None of the above

459. What does the Good Friday Agreement guarantee?

    A. Protection of minority rights in Northern Ireland and Ireland

    B. Equal voting rights among the Irish and the Northern Irish

    C. Freedom of religion

    D. None of the above

460. How has the Good Friday Agreement affected politics in Northern Ireland since 1998?

    A. It has resulted in more violence between Catholics and Protestants

    B. It has helped create stability between unionists and nationalists

    C. It has led to increased tensions between the two sides

    D. It has had no impact on politics in Northern Ireland

Answers

451. A. A peace agreement signed in 1998 to end conflict between Ireland and Northern Ireland

452. A. Representatives of the Irish Republican Army (IRA), loyalist paramilitary organizations, and representatives from Britain, Europe, and the US State Department

453. A. The end of sectarian violence in Northern Ireland

454. B. Belfast, Northern Ireland

455. B. The Belfast Agreement

456. C. Former First Minister of Northern Ireland David Trimble

457. C. April 10, 1998

458. A. It was an important step toward peace in Northern Ireland

459. A. Protection of minority rights in Northern Ireland and Ireland

460. B. It has helped create stability between unionists and nationalists

Modern Britain (2000s–present)

Welcome to modern Britain! In the 2000s, life in Britain has drastically changed. People travel faster and connect globally with new technologies such as smartphones and high-speed internet. Businesses have grown bigger, cities are much more diverse, and people enjoy a variety of cultures. Despite these changes, traditional British values remain, such as politeness, punctuality, and respect for other people's beliefs. Come explore this exciting new era of Britain with us!

461. What is the capital of England?

    A. London

    B. Manchester

    C. Birmingham

    D. Liverpool

462. Which is not a member state of the United Kingdom?

    A. Wales

    B. Northern Ireland

    C. Scotland

    D. Ireland

463. Who was prime minister from 2007-2010?

    A. Gordon Brown

    B. Tony Blair

    C. David Cameron

    D. Theresa May

464. Alongside which two other countries did Britain join the European Union?

    A. Norway and Sweden

    B. Spain and Greece

    C. Ireland and Poland

    D. Denmark and Ireland

465. Who became prime minister of the UK in 2010?

    A. Tony Blair

    B. David Cameron

    C. Liz Truss

    D. Boris Johnson

466. How many members of Parliament are there in Britain?

    A. 500

    B. 650

    C. 750

    D. 900

467. In what year did same-sex marriage become legal in the UK?

    A. 2010

    B. 2013

    C. 2014

    D. 2016

468. What was the national anthem of England until 2022?

    A. "Land of Hope and Glory"

    B. "God Save The Queen"

    C. "Rule Britannia"

    D. "Jerusalem"

469. Who became the prime minister of the UK in October 2022?

    A. Rishi Sunak

    B. David Cameron

    C. Gordon Brown

    D. Tony Blair

470. What type of government does Britain have?

    A. Republic

    B. Constitutional monarchy

    C. Democracy

    D. Autocracy

471. When did the Scottish Independence Referendum take place?

    A. 2007

    B. 2010

    C. 2014

    D. 2019

472. What is the official religion of England?

    A. Anglicanism

    B. Catholicism

    C. Lutheranism

    D. None of the above

473. How many members are there in the House of Lords?

    A. 800

    B. 950

    C. 1100

    D. The number changes

474. Who is responsible for making laws in Britain?

    A. Prime minister

    B. Parliament

    C. Queen

    D. Citizens

475. Which color does not appear on the British flag?

    A. Blue

    B. Red

    C. White

    D. Green

476. In what year did the Conservative Party fail to secure the majority in Parliament, leading to first hung Parliament since 1974?

    A. 2001

    B. 2010

    C. 2014

    D. 2005

477. When did the British government hold a referendum to leave the European Union?

    A. 2010

    B. 2012

    C. 2014

    D. 2016

478. What is the main currency in Britain?

    A. Euro

    B. Pound sterling

    C. Dollar

    D. Mark

479. Who was the prime minister at the time of the Brexit referendum?

    A. Theresa May

    B. Gordon Brown

    C. David Cameron

    D. Tony Blair

480. Approximately what percentage of voters voted for Brexit?

    A. 48 percent

    B. 52 percent

    C. 59 percent

    D. 61 percent

481. Who became the leader of the Conservative Party in 2019?

    A. Theresa May

    B. David Cameron

    C. Boris Johnson

    D. Rishi Sunak

482. What animal appears on British coins and notes?

    A. Lion

    B. Fox

    C. Bull

    D. Eagle

483. When was the Scottish Parliament established?

    A. 1999

    B. 2003

    C. 2005

    D. 2007

484. What is the population of Scotland as of 2019?

    A. four million

    B. five million

    C. eight million

    D. ten million

485. Who was the prime minister during the 2003 invasion of Iraq?

    A. David Cameron

    B. John Major

    C. Gordon Brown

    D. Tony Blair

486. When were the "7/7" bombings carried out in London?

    A. 2001

    B. 2002

    C. 2005

    D. 2007

487. How many members are there in the House of Commons?

    A. 500

    B. 650

    C. 750

    D. 900

488. What color appears on British passport covers?

    A. Blue

    B. Red

    C. White

    D. Green

489. Who is the current prime minister in Scotland?

    A. Nicola Sturgeon

    B. David Cameron

    C. Alex Salmond

    D. John Swinney

490. Who was the most recent female prime minister of Britain?

    A. Margaret Thatcher

    B. Ursula von der Leyen

    C. Liz Truss

    D. None of the above

Answers

461. A. London
462. D. Ireland
463. A. Gordon Brown
464. D. Denmark and Ireland
465. B. David Cameron
466. B. 650
467. B. 2013
468. B. "God Save The Queen"
469. A. Rishi Sunak
470. B. Constitutional monarchy
471. C. 2014
472. A. Anglicanism
473. D. The number changes
474. B. Parliament
475. D. Green
476. B. 2010
477. D. 2016
478. B. Pound sterling
479. C. David Cameron
480. B. 52 percent
481. C. Boris Johnson
482. A. Lion
483. A. 1999
484. B. five million
485. D. Tony Blair
486. C. 2005
487. B. 650
488. A. Blue
489. D. John Swinney
490. C. Liz Truss

Coronation of King Charles III (2023)

Everyone in the kingdom gathered around to witness the coronation of King Charles III. Music filled the air as people cheered and celebrated his becoming king. He made his way through an archway of decorated flags, with a crown atop his head. All eyes were on him as he took his place on the throne under a royal canopy made from velvet and jewels. The celebration marked a new beginning for their beloved country, and all rejoiced at this momentous occasion!

491. Who crowned King Charles III as monarch of the United Kingdom?

   A. Prince William

   B. Archbishop of Canterbury

   C. Queen Elizabeth II

   D. Prime Minister Liz Truss

492. What were some elements included in the coronation ceremony for King Charles III?

   A. Sword and scepter

   B. Blessing from God

   C. Oath to protect Britain

   D. All of the above

493. How many people attended the coronation ceremony for King Charles III?

    A. 1,500

    B. More than 2,000

    C. 700

    D. 1,000

494. Which two members of the royal family stood with King Charles III during the coronation ceremony?

    A. Prince William and Queen Elizabeth II

    B. Princess Anne and Prince Harry

    C. Prince William and Queen Camilla

    D. Duke of Edinburgh and Duchess of Cornwall

495. Who wrote the prayer recited at the coronation ceremony for King Charles III?

    A. Archbishop Justin Welby

    B. Prime Minister Theresa May

    C. King George VI

    D. Queen Victoria

496. What type of traditional musical performances were performed by the Bands Of His Majesty's Royal Marines?

    A. Jazz music

    B. Classical or traditional music

    C. Rock music

    D. Pop music

497. What is a new role given to King Charles III as part ruler of the realm?

    A. Head of government

    B. Head of state

    C. Commander in chief

    D. Ambassador for the UK

498. What was the name of King Charles III's coronation anthem?

A. "God Save Our Gracious King"

B. "Rule Britannia"

C. "Crown Him With Many Crowns"

D. "Jerusalem"

499. Who led the recitation at the coronation ceremony for King Charles III?

A. Archbishop Justin Welby

B. Queen Elizabeth II

C. Prince William

D. Prime Minister Theresa May

500. Who gave a speech in honor of King Charles III during his coronation ceremony?

A. Archbishop Justin Welby

B. Queen Elizabeth II

C. Prince William

D. Prime Minister Theresa May

Answers

491. B. Archbishop of Canterbury
492. D. All of the above
493. B. More than 2,000
494. C. Prince William and Queen Camilla
495. A. Archbishop Justin Welby
496. B. Classical or traditional music
497. B. Head of state
498. A. "God Save Our Gracious King"
499. A. Archbishop Justin Welby
500. C. Prince William

Conclusion

The history of England is a long and winding trail full of surprises. From the days when English kings reigned over an island nation to today's diverse cultural landscape, this country has been through many changes. It has had its share of great leaders and notorious villains who have all left their mark on modern-day Britain.

England has seen significant social change throughout its past, from the Industrial Revolution, which brought sweeping technological advancements that transformed life for millions, to more recent events such as Brexit, which will shape British politics for years or even decades to come. No matter how much changes, however, certain constants remain: England's commitment to democracy and human rights and her fierce sense of justice tempered by mercy and compassion toward others less fortunate. These values are what truly define the British people regardless of their ethnic or religious backgrounds or political opinions.

Britain may be small, but it continuously plays a notable role on the world stage. Through its economic power, global influence, and strong cultural heritage, it has earned a unique place in history as one of Europe's most prominent countries. Its future may be uncertain, but England's past is an inspiring legacy to follow—one that will continue to shape lives for generations to come.

Check out another book in the series

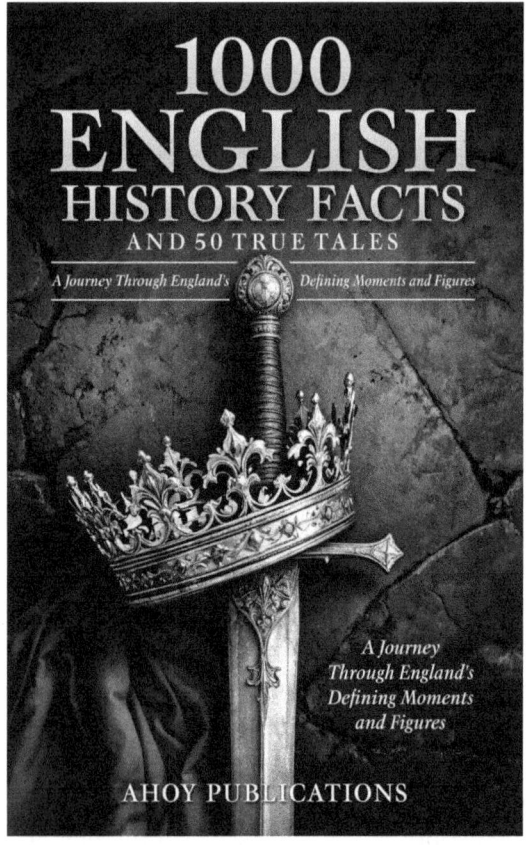

Welcome Aboard, Check Out This Limited-Time Free Bonus!

Ahoy, reader! Welcome to the Ahoy Publications family, and thanks for snagging a copy of this book! Since you've chosen to join us on this journey, we'd like to offer you something special.

Check out the link below for a FREE e-book filled with delightful facts about American History.

But that's not all - you'll also have access to our exclusive email list with even more free e-books and insider knowledge. Well, what are ye waiting for? Click the link below to join and set sail toward exciting adventures in American History.

Access your bonus here

https://ahoypublications.com/

Or, Scan the QR code!

Sources and Additional References

Schama, Simon. *A History of Britain: At the Edge of the World? 3000 BC-AD 1603*. New York: Hyperion, 2000.

Ackroyd, Peter. *Foundation: The History of England from Its Earliest Beginnings to the Tudors*. New York: Thomas Dunne Books, 2011.

Douglas, David C., and George W. Greenaway, eds. *English Historical Documents*. London: Eyre & Spottiswoode, various volumes and years.

Elton, G. R. *England Under the Tudors*. London: Methuen, 1955.

Fraser, Antonia. *The Lives of the Kings and Queens of England*. Berkeley: University of California Press, 1975.